Paper Sculpture

1. The Author

Paper Sculpture
step by step

ELIZABETH PETHERBRIDGE

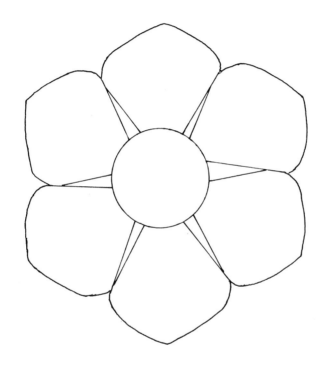

LONDON : G. BELL AND SONS

*Printed in Great Britain by litho
by Anchor Press, and bound by Wm. Brendon,
both of Tiptree, Essex*
ISBN 0 7135 1718 2

Contents

Photographs

                    (*Photographs are by Photoscript, East Molesey, Surrey*)

Foreword

The origins of paper sculpture are to be found in the ancient oriental paper crafts which were used in the main as decorations for religious festivals.

In more recent times its use has spread to Europe and America principally as a medium for display and advertising. Its unique effect still has the value of being considered somewhat unusual and therefore eyecatching.

My own interest in paper sculpture began when I was asked to find a demonstrator for a talk with the aim of improving display and the techniques involved.

Such a person, it seemed, was nowhere to be found but my curiosity was aroused and was kindled when I found a book on the subject.

Armed with this, I began tentatively my first piece and after much trial and error a rather comical lamb emerged complete with a 'woolly' curled coat.

Thus began a most intriguing and satisfying hobby and, as one of the main reasons for writing this book is to encourage others to take up this absorbing pastime, I would stress that I have no background of art training.

In this book only the fringe of the subject has been touched, for in paper anything is possible. By following through the exercises and patterns readers should be well able to progress through the book and then branch out with their own creations.

All that beginners need is a fund of patience and an ability to use their fingers.

Paper sculpture is great fun but it does help if you have an understanding family who keep out of the way when things are not going right!

Sanderstead, 1972   Elizabeth Petherbridge

Equipment

This is basically a very inexpensive craft as the tools are for the most part found in the home. Some are only occasionally used while a few become firm favourites.

BOARD

A firm board approximately 24″ × 24″, to protect the table or work surface from being damaged by scoring. Cover this with several layers of flat newspaper then a thick smooth sheet of brown paper on top. This will prevent the newsprint from spoiling the white paper. After a certain amount of scoring and cutting these papers must be replaced or the rough surface will spoil the work.

SCISSORS

A variety of sizes are used from large blades to fine curved nail scissors. Do keep them sharp or they will roughen the edges.

KNIVES

A comfortable handle and a short sharp blade makes the most satisfactory tool. A stencil knife, craft knife, balsa wood knife, general-purpose knife to name a few are all pleasant to work with. A large-handled trimming knife is invaluable for cutting card. Again it is essential to keep the blades sharp. Several types carry spare blades in the handles. Keep them carefully in their box so the blades do not suffer, or cause, damage.

ADHESIVES

Bostick No. 1 has been used for the main part in this book, the special shaped cap being extremely useful when spreading glue over an area.

Uhu is another good clear instant glue.

Copydex can be used when there is not a strain on the paper.

Double-sided sticky tape is invaluable at times, also Selo-tape though this does discolour and can peel.

STAPLER

Not an essential item but can be very useful, either the large office type which opens on a hinge or the small hand type.

RULERS

A steel ruler is a must for scoring or cutting with a knife, as the blade plays havoc with a wooden or plastic one. Keep these for measuring and bending only.

PENCILS

An H.B. for preference of good quality. Always use it lightly and well sharpened. Keep a spare one handy.

MISCELLANEOUS

A good-quality soft rubber and the round flat typewriter eraser removes the mistaken blob of glue. An assortment of paper clips and fasteners, compass, pair of dividers, tweezers, set square, french curves (for making scrolls and curved shapes). Even the spring type clothes peg has its uses. A handy damp cloth to wipe the fingers.

PAPER

It is a mistaken economy to get cheap paper. Get the best possible. A firm rough-textured water colour or cartridge paper gives the best results. The cheaper thinner types tear and crease easily, quickly spoiling the whole appearance of the work.

Cartridge paper can be obtained in many colours and is coloured all through so will not be marred by scoring. Foil-covered or painted card shows white after being scored.

Sugar paper is useless as it has no body.

CARDBOARD

Ivory cardboard for a lightweight and mounting card for a heavier quality. For some large items the sides of a package carton can be used but it must be firm.

The knives can be purchased from hardware, Do It Yourself or model shops and stationers. The latter can sometimes produce good paper, but usually it is best to go to a good art supplier.

In London—Paper Chase in Tottenham Court Road and Kettles of Holborn both carry an excellent selection of all types of paper.

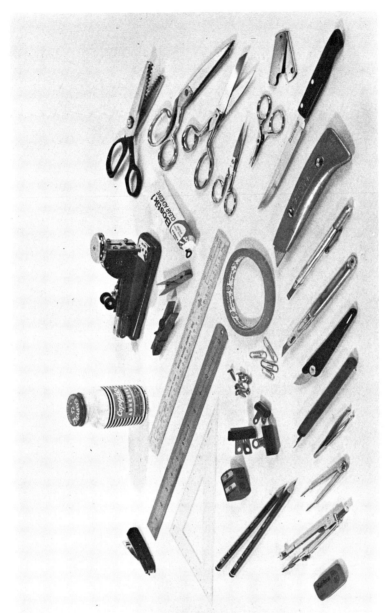

2. Equipment

Useful Tips

Any Deviation from the Scoring Lines given in these Patterns will alter the Shape.

In making cones, cylinders and tubes, glue and overlap the edges then lay the seam down on the work surface and pressing firmly slide the fingers inside along the seam.

Use a pair of dividers to score a circle. Put one point in the centre and score with the other.

Cut towards angles from both sides to meet at the point. This prevents the paper being torn by turning the scissors here.

When working under curves pull the ends inwards a little to make the fold more firm.

A spiral of paper can be formed by pulling a narrow strip of paper between the rounded edge of the scissors blade and the thumb, with the left hand twisting away from the body.

A dab of glue at the end of a small strip of paper will slip under awkward places needing to be stuck.

14

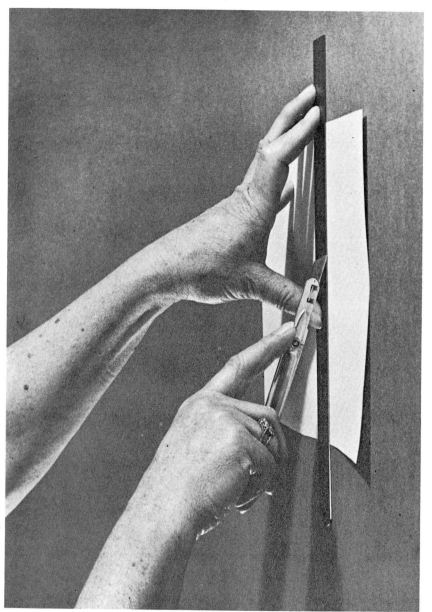

3. Scoring

1: Techniques

SCORING & FOLDING

Scoring is making a minute incision with a sharp knife as it is drawn across the paper. This allows the cut edges to part and so permit a crisp neat fold. Always score on the side of the paper that is to be bent away, as otherwise the fold will not be crisp.

Use a steel ruler and holding it firmly in place draw the knife along it using very light pressure. It is essential to find the right pressure as not enough makes a messy fold, but too much cuts the paper in two! The correct pressure will ensure that the lines and curves 'crack' easily and that the models are crisp and clean. Remember the less pieces are handled the better the finish.

After scoring a line down a strip of paper hold the piece in both hands either side of the line. With the thumbs parallel to the score line bend the paper away. Work along the line, then fold it together and pull the fold between the fingers and thumb.

To judge the importance of scoring try folding a piece of paper by merely pressing along the edges, then score another piece and compare the difference.

BENDING

This method gives a rounded effect to the paper.

Place the paper on the table holding it down tightly with the edge of a ruler and use the other hand to draw the paper upwards from under the ruler at an angle of about 45°. As seen in photograph 4.

For a more pronounced curve draw the paper closer to the ruler.

Larger pieces can be curved by holding the short edges in each hand and pulling the paper down over the edge of a table several times.

These methods result in the surface of the paper being 'damaged' or softened and so causes the reverse side, which is now stronger, to push the weak side over.

Alternatively the method can be used to straighten paper that has been rolled too tightly.

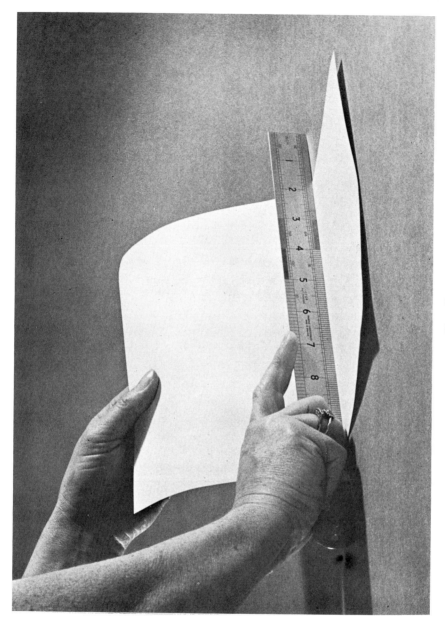

4. Bending

Small tubes can be made first by bending and then wrapping them round a smooth pencil or piece of dowel.

CURLING

This is done with the blade of a pair of large scissors or a knife and is for small pieces such as leaves, petals or the hair of figures. The action is shown in photograph 5.

Open the scissors wide holding them with the thumb resting on the cutting blade. Hold a strip of paper between the thumb and the blade, and use the left hand to pull it, at the same time curving the right hand away to ensure that the strip of paper is in contact with the cutting edge throughout its length.

Practice is essential to find the correct pressure for both the thumb and the pull.

When curling a row of strips always keep a tight hold on the upper end of the strip to prevent the risk of a tear.

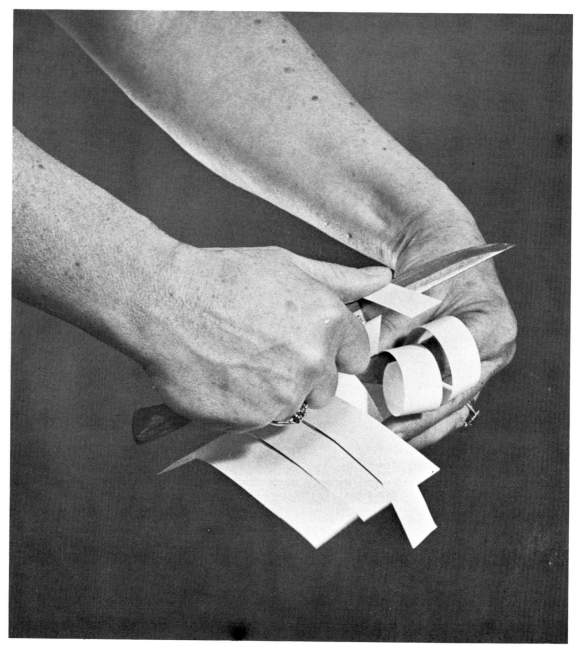

5. Curling

CUTTING
With a Knife
The observation of a few basic rules will save much time and make for easier working.

A sheet of glass is the ideal cutting base as the surface rarely gets spoilt, but it needs practice to become expert on the slippery surface and it is best to start with a softer cutting base.

To protect the table or work top use a piece of firm board 24″ × 24″ and cover this with several sheets of flat newspaper. Then put on top a sheet of clean un-creased brown paper to protect the white paper from the newsprint.

Place the steel ruler on a piece of cartridge paper and hold it firmly in place as even the slightest movement will spoil the cutting line.

Hold the knife comfortably but not too tightly. With the maximum amount of the blade in contact with the paper draw the knife down towards the body. Do not use the tip of the blade only as this will ruin the blade.

Do not try to cut cardboard with one stroke of the knife as this can not only be extremely tiring but jagged edges will result. Keep the ruler firmly in place and repeat the cuts several times always drawing the knife carefully towards the body until the card is cut. A few extra strokes may be needed at the beginning and end.

With Scissors
When cutting a curved edge to prevent a jagged edge always hold the scissors in an upright position turning only the paper and NOT the scissors.

Practice with large scissors held in a vertical position. Open them wide and place the paper right into the base of the blades. Slowly close the scissors and with the left hand feed the paper, following the pencilled curve to the left or right.

It is advisable to cut a rough margin to begin with as it is difficult to follow the curve with too much paper falling away.

2: Shaping the Paper

There are only four basic methods of shaping the paper. These are scoring, folding, bending and curling. Each is very simple and it is the ingenuity with which they can be utilised to make simple or complex structures that makes paper sculpture so fascinating. The varying effects of light and shade, ranging from the sharp contrasts of the folds to the softness of the curves, gives a dimensional beauty unique to this art form.

Everything has to be stylised as the true nature forms cannot be reproduced in this media. The forms are very much simplified keeping only the main essential lines and discarding the rest. For instance with leaves only the main veins are depicted and the folds in cloth are very much reduced. In the case of small faces it is often best just to cut the features and not to add additional pieces.

Paper sculpture in the round is the most difficult form as it has to be seen from all sides. It must be built up over a wired or wooden structure which is fixed into a firm block at the base. A simpler way is to use a series of cones and cylinders as these are very firm and make a good base to build upon.

Half relief is only seen from the front and must have a cardboard structure which is covered with various shaped, scored and bowed pieces of paper. These are fixed by tabs and are gradually built up to give an appearance of solidity. This is then fixed to a background or is given a back support.

In making an original design, so much paper will be wasted before the desired shape is evolved that reams of beautiful paper would be discarded. It is therefore better to use paper from old company reports or minutes or even the pages from glossy magazines. Whatever is used must have 'body' and be firm enough to stand up to considerable handling. Here it is a question of patience and of try, try, try again until the needed score or crease comes in just the right place. Some elaborate items may take a week or more to work out but when they do the feeling of elation is exhilarating and makes it all worth while.

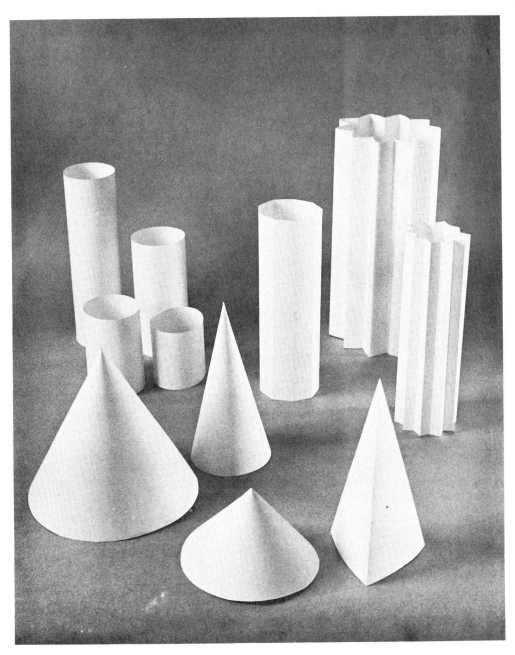

6. Simple shapes—cones and cylinders

SIMPLE SHAPES

Scoring gives strength. Hold a piece of paper horizontally in one hand and it will droop, the same will happen if it is stood on end. But score a line down the centre, fold along the length, open out the paper and it will now hold both positions.

A smooth cylinder of paper will crumple under weight. But score the paper on alternate sides, pleat it, then overlap and glue the edges together and the cylinder will now have rigidity.

Such cylinders can be used to make attractive and economical items of display equipment. Two cylinders can be joined by a cardboard or even a pleated shelf.

A cylinder scored on one side only will give the impression of a Grecian column.

A PLEATED CYLINDER

Measure a piece of paper 12″×9″. On one side of the paper lightly mark with a pencil 1-inch intervals across the top and bottom of the paper. With a steel ruler and a sharp knife join the marks with a scoring line.

Fold all these lines, then turn the paper over marking half an inch between the lines already made. Score as before and fold these lines. Now pleat up the paper alternately folding along the lines. See diagram 1.

SCORING LINES   PLEATED CYLINDER
                                                 CIRCLE
                                                 FAN

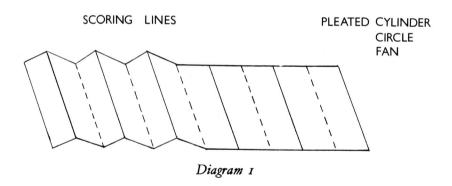

Diagram 1

CONES

Cones form the basis of many models. They also have strength and can be plain, pleated or pyramid in shape. A cone is made from a section of a circle with the radius of the circle controlling the height of the cone.

To make up a plain cone cut $\frac{3}{4}$ of a circle as in diagram 2. For easier manipulation bend the paper by pulling it under a ruler as previously described. It will help to improve the apex of the cone if the paper is made pliable by gently pulling the point two or three times under the ruler and then by see-sawing it up and down with the straight edges held in each hand, working the paper towards the point.

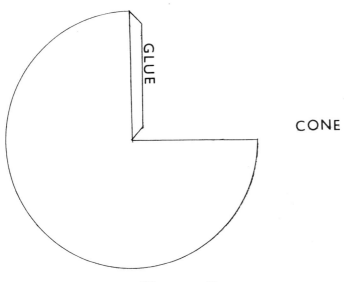

GLUE

CONE

Diagram 2. Cone

To complete the cone glue the tab and fix under the opposite edge. Lay the cone seam side down and press a finger along the seam and a pencil into the point. It is not always necessary to have a tab, as the two straight edges of a cone can be overlapped easily.

A slimmer cone needs less and a wider cone more of a circle.

For a pleated cone use almost the whole circle. A pyramid cone—diagram 3— is made by dividing the section of the circle into equal parts. Score the solid lines on the right side and cut straight edges as indicated by the dotted lines.

Fold the sections, glue the tab and fix under the opposite edge.

24

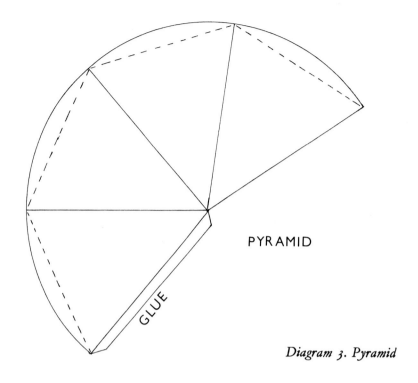

PYRAMID

GLUE

Diagram 3. Pyramid

SCORING A CURVE

Take a rectangular piece of paper about 12″×6″ and very lightly pencil the dotted line in diagram 4.

SCORING A CURVE

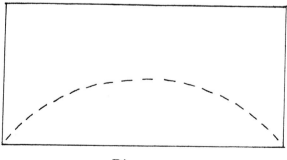

Diagram 4

Turning the paper whilst scoring makes a smooth curve. First practise just turning the paper by spreading the left hand under the curve, as in photographs 7 and 8, and pressing with the finger pads. Sometimes the paper has to be rotated in fairly large circles against the brown paper first to get a 'sheen' between the papers.

Having got the paper to turn, then, using the index finger of the right hand, follow the score line whilst the left hand turns the paper in the opposite direction. Repeat this several times to get the feel of the action. Then score with the knife. Whereas it is possible to retrace a straight line it is virtually impossible to do so in a curve.

Always work the fold underneath the arch of the curve. Hold the end of the curve in both hands placing the thumbs either side of the score line and bend the paper away.

Then, as in photograph 9, hold the upper edge above the curve in the left hand, placing the other under the lower edge with the thumb in front and the fingers spread out behind the paper. Gently press the fingers and thumb together at the same time slightly turning the wrist. If the scoring is correct the fold goes easily round the curve with no further movement. Repeat the process at the other end of the curve. NEVER pull down the upper edge of the paper or it will crumple.

Pull the ends of the curves together and see how very different the flat piece of paper is now.

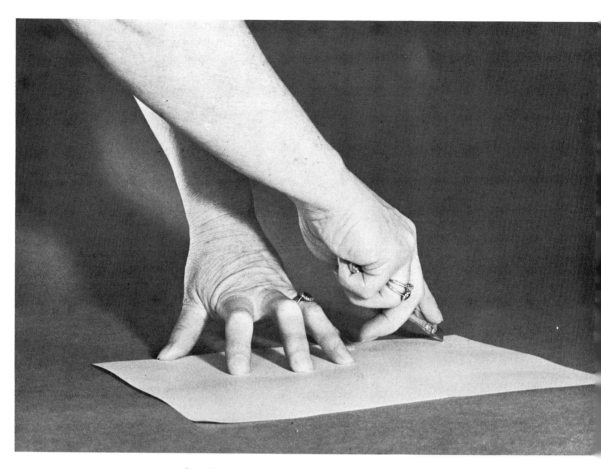

7. Scoring a curve: position of the hands, start

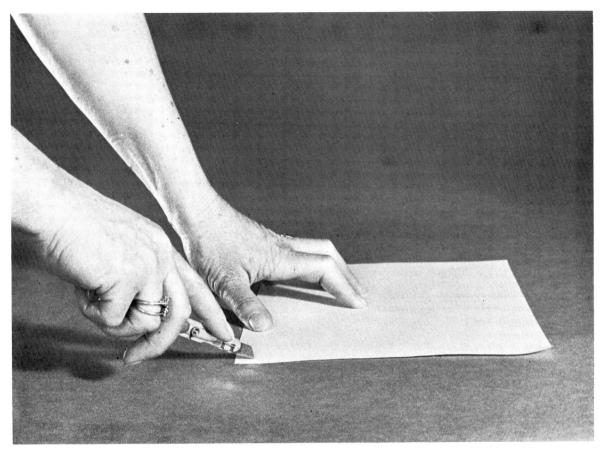

8. Scoring a curve: position of the hands, finish

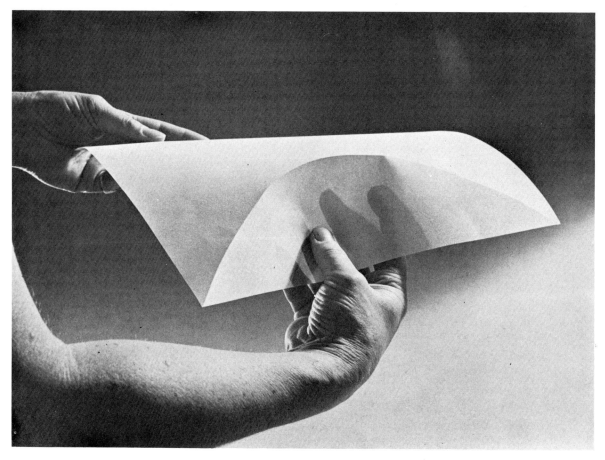

9. Scoring a curve: position of the hands, folding

SCORING A CIRCLE

All circles must have a section removed to get the scored line to fold. The larger the section removed the greater the depth of the fold.

Try first with diagram 5. Draw the circle with a compass, then instead of using a pencil for the second circle, use a pair of dividers. Put one point in the centre and the other is used to score the circle. Thus a smooth circle is easily achieved.

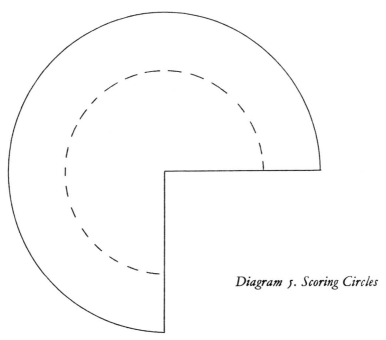

Diagram 5. Scoring Circles

Work as for the curve by bending the fold at the end of the score using both hands. Then only holding the outer edge work with the other hand under the curve.

Now try diagram 6, scoring the inner circles on alternate sides of the paper.

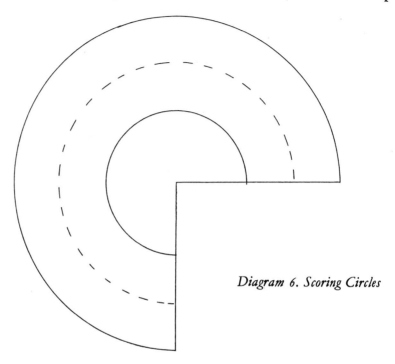

Diagram 6. Scoring Circles

The finished shapes are seen in photograph 10.

SCORING EXERCISES (Diagrams 7 to 10)

1. Draw the pattern onto a piece of paper roughly the same size as the page. Do NOT CUT yet as the extra paper is needed for turning whilst the curve is being scored.

Score on the right side starting at the point following the curve to the inner cut.

Now cut out remembering to keep the scissors upright and only turning the paper.

Start to fold in the centre and work to the point first, then working under the curve to the other end. When complete gently pull the rounded cut section towards the score line.

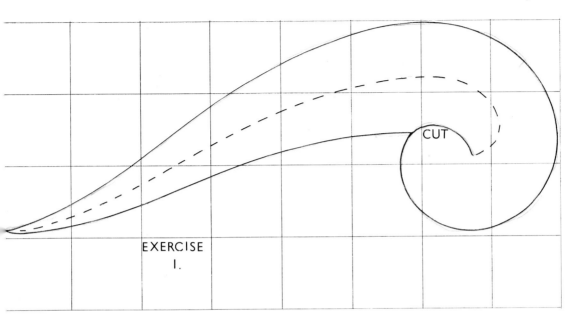

Diagram 7

2. Draw the pattern and work as before. Bend the fold along the straighter section and work to the points not forgetting to work under the curve.

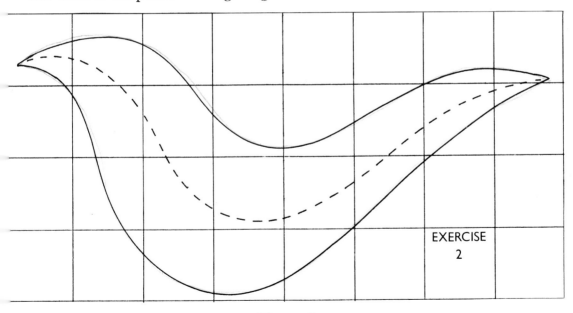

Diagram 8

3. Repeat the process as before bending the fold along the centre, work half way round the curve. Then bend the fold at the point and, if the scoring is correct, just by pulling, the point in the curve will fold round.

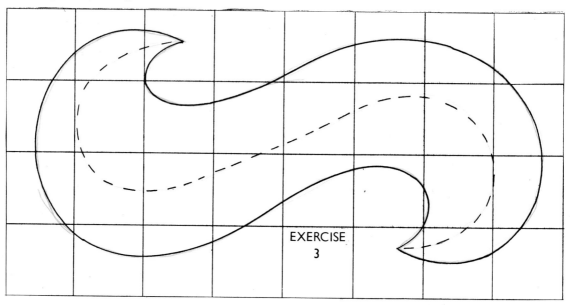

Diagram 9

4. Draw the pattern and score the dotted lines on the right side starting at the point. Then turn the paper over and score the solid centre line. Cut out the shape and bend the paper on alternate sides, working under the curves and pulling the points over.

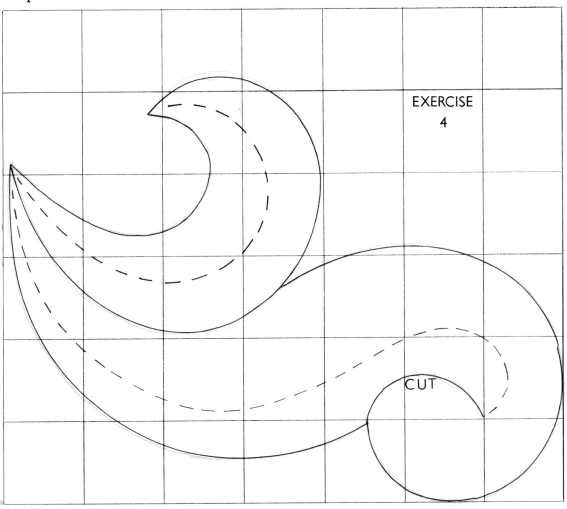

EXERCISE

4

CUT

Diagram 10

Repeat these exercises until the movements are easy, then try to score freehand without a pencil.

10. Circles and first exercises

3: Patterns to Make

CLEMATIS (Diagram 11)

All flowers made in paper sculpture are very stylised as the nature of the paper prevents a true likeness to all the many intricacies of a real flower.

This pattern is very simple and makes an effective design. Cut out the flower pattern and cut the solid lines in the petals. Score the dotted lines on the wrong side. With a ruler, on the right side, curl each petal from the centre line to the outer edges.

Stamen

With a compass make a circle with a radius of $\frac{3}{4}''$. Cut all round very finely to within $\frac{1}{4}''$ of the centre. Then very carefully with a ruler gently curl the stamens to the centre on the right side. Glue the stamens to the centre of the flower.

Leaf

Cut out the pattern but vary the size for interest. Curl the leaves on the wrong side from the centre to the outer edges. Fix the flowers and leaves to a background with small dabs of glue.

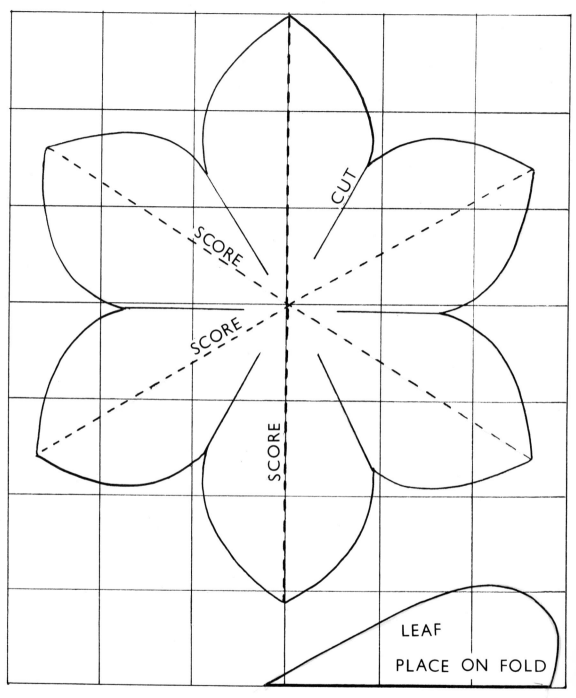

Diagram 11. Clematis

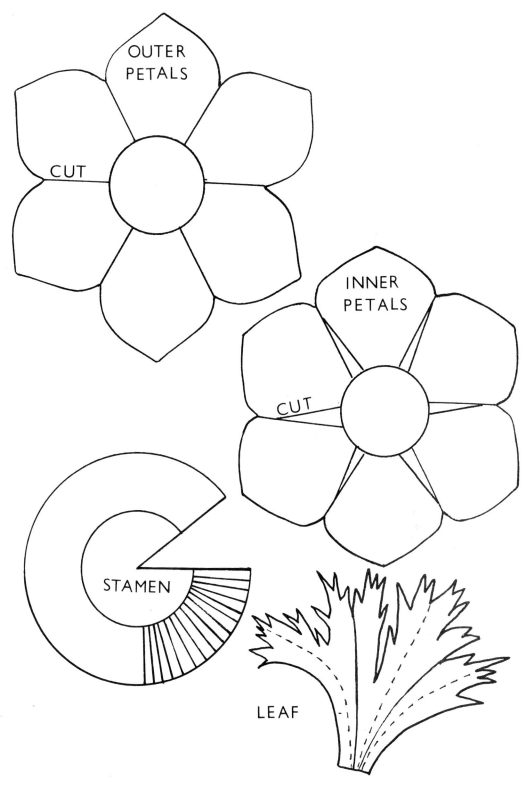

OUTER
PETALS

CUT

INNER
PETALS

CUT

STAMEN

LEAF

Diagram 12. Anemone

ANEMONE (Diagrams 12 and 13)

Cut out the outer petal pattern as indicated separating the petals by cutting the solid lines to the centre circle. Do the same with the inner petals but this time cutting two lines to the centre circle. On the right side, curl gently with your ruler from the base of the petal giving extra pressure at the tip. Vary this whether you want the flowers opened or closed.

Put a dab of glue behind the centre of the inner petals and place over the outer section making sure the petals are off set as in photograph 11.

Cut out the stamen section cutting to the centre on the long solid lines. Score the centre circle on the wrong side, then cut small strips in the outer ring as part shown in the pattern. On the right side sharply bend the outer ends of the stamens with your scissors. Make a cone shape in the centre by overlapping the straight edges about ½". Glue. Place on the table cone uppermost and gently press the stamens up round the cone. Glue to the centre of the inner petals.

The stems are made by cutting a slightly curved strip ½" wide which is scored down the centre. As the flower head is rather heavy, it is advisable to fix a piece of wire inside the crease. At the top of the stem cut down four or six small strips for almost ½". Bend these back and glue behind the flower being careful not to close the fold of the stem. See diagram 13.

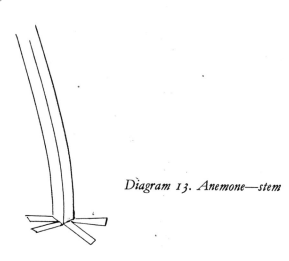

Diagram 13. Anemone—stem

Cut the leaf pattern and score the dotted lines on the right side and the solid ones on the wrong. Cut three leaves to each flower varying the shapes a little. Glue one either side of the stem fixing the third in the opening. For a fully opened flower the leaves are fixed about one inch below the petals.

11. Clematis and anemones in a tankard

ROSE & LEAF (Diagram 14)
Rose

Cut out the pattern and curl to the centre with scissors. Roll the long strip tightly for a few turns, then make looser turns with the rest of the paper around the tighter roll. Work it around to get the shape required. If necessary put a dab of glue on the round base and press the centre of the rose onto this. Hold until dry to keep the rose in the desired shape. Place in position by putting a small dab of glue where the petals touch the background or each other.

Leaf

Cut out the shape given and score down the centre on the reverse side, curving the line slightly to give a more interesting shape. Bend with the ruler on the reverse side from the centre vein to the outer edges. To give greater detail the edges can be serrated. Fix to the background.

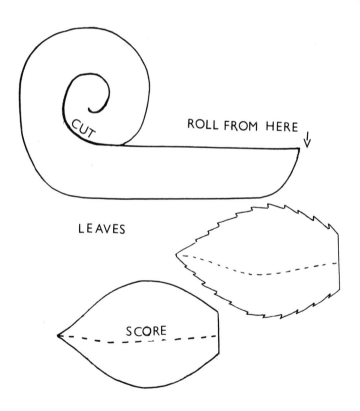

Diagram 14. Rose & Leaf

TANKARD (Diagrams 15 and 16)
Base Circle

With a compass and a radius of $2\frac{3}{4}''$ draw a circle ($5\frac{1}{2}''$ across). Inside this draw another circle radius $2\frac{1}{2}''$, and another one of $2\frac{1}{4}''$.

Cut away a quarter of the circle as shown in diagram 15. Score the middle circle on the right side and the inner one on the reverse. Fold the score lines as shown in the exercise on page 30. Overlap the straight edges by $\frac{1}{4}''$ at the outer edge and glue.

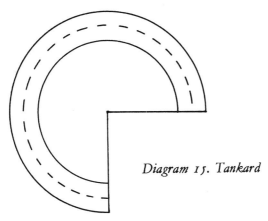

Diagram 15. Tankard

Main Tankard Pattern

Do NOT PLACE THE PATTERN ON A FOLD, but trace round and keeping the centre line turn the pattern and trace the other half. With a knife cut the four horizontal lines. Cut out the pattern and bend along the length on the wrong side with a ruler. Roll and join the seam WITH PAPER CLIPS. Place over the base ring and adjust the seam so the tankard fits closely round the inner scoring. Glue the seam. Dab a little glue in a few places under the base rim of the tankard, fix onto the base circle and hold until dry.

Top Rim

With a compass and a radius of $1\frac{3}{4}''$ draw a circle. Draw another inside this with a radius of $1\frac{1}{2}''$ and finally one of $1\frac{1}{4}''$. Score the middle circle on the right side. Cut through the rim and round the inner circle so removing the centre. Overlap the rim until it covers the top of the tankard. Glue in place.

Handle

Cut out the pattern scoring the dotted lines on the right side, and cutting all the small solid lines. Bend back the outer edge at right angles. Glue the corners and overlap the ends where the line curves. Cut and bend the inner edges. Cut a strip of paper $\frac{1}{4}''$ wide and long enough to go round the outside and the inside of the handle. Glue this along the tabs to keep them at right angles. Leave about $\frac{1}{4}''$ extra at each end. Slip these into the slots on the tankard. Glue them on the inside and press them against the inner wall of the tankard.

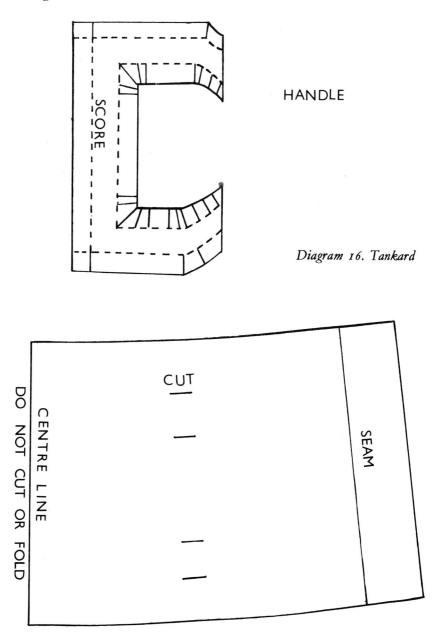

HANDLE

Diagram 16. Tankard

DISPLAY STANDS (Diagram 17)

These are simple and effective as supports for photographs, notices, books, visual-aids, embroidery, cushions or toys.

Stand A can be made of cartridge paper, although a light-weight card will be firmer. A folded post-card makes a small neat stand.

Cut out the pattern placing the edge on a fold as shown. Open out and support the notice on the angled sections.

Stand B is made in a very firm mounting card. At the base it has an extra area on which to stand a book or display box. Trace round the pattern and cut with a trimming knife against a steel ruler. Glue or staple the reinforced strip along the base as shown. Place a strip of masking tape down the back while the stand is folded to strengthen the fold line.

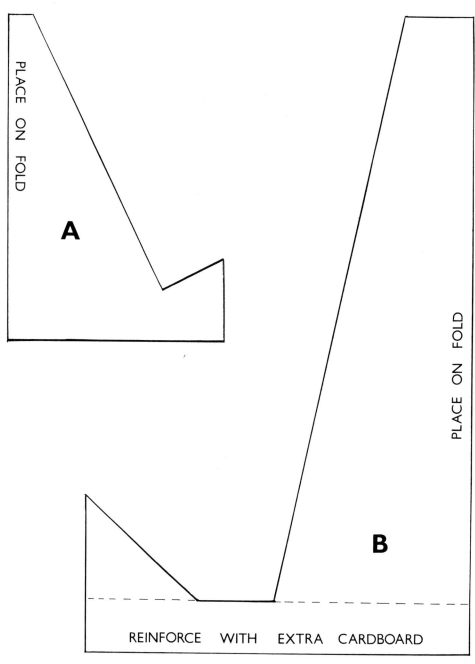

PLACE ON FOLD

A

PLACE ON FOLD

B

REINFORCE WITH EXTRA CARDBOARD

Diagram 17. Display Stands

12. Display stands

(By permission of *Home and Country*)

13. 21st key, shield and horseshoe

21ST KEY (Diagram 18)

Cut out the main section of the pattern and score all the lines indicated, the dotted lines on the right side, and the solid ones at the top of the key blade A–A and the base of the figure two, on the reverse. Cut the small lines shown. On the right side fold the main stem of the key overlapping the outer edges underneath, gluing them together.

Glue the lower edges of the key blade together. Bend the two tabs marked X underneath the tip of the stem and glue together. Do not place the handle on a fold. Trace round the pattern keeping the centre line; reverse the pattern and trace again. Score on the right side. Cut through the rim—marked on the pattern—to remove the centre of the handle. Make a small nick at the end of the stem in the top crease and another in the middle of the glued seam below. Insert the tab into the stem so that the handle just slips into the nicks. A small dab of glue at the back will keep it secure.

Cut and score the figures as shown. Make two incisions in the top crease of the stem and slip the long tabs in. To avoid any glue showing fold a small strip of paper, gluing both sides. Then slip between the figures and the incision at the back.

The numerals can be altered to 18.

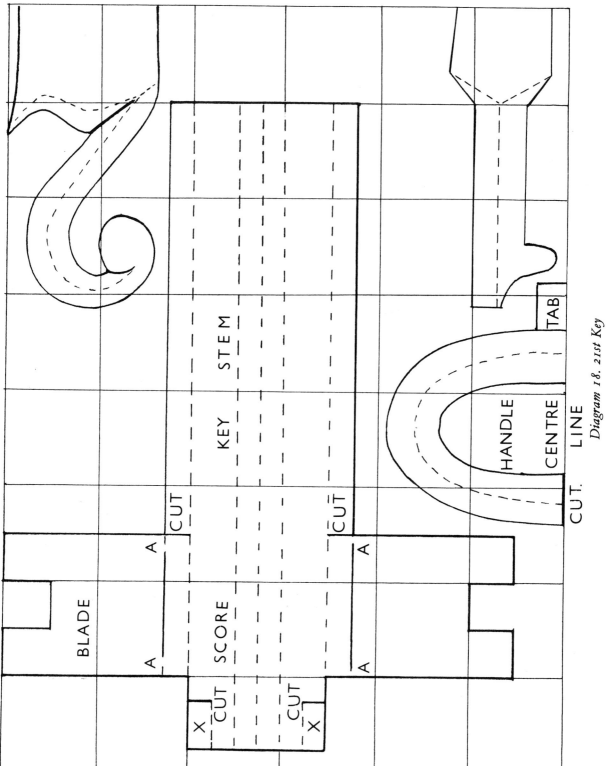

Diagram 18. 21st Key

SHIELD (Diagrams 19 to 21)

Cut out the pattern and score the dotted lines on the right side. Cut the small solid lines in the border. Fold the border back at right angles. Overlap and glue the corners at the top of the shield—as a box lid. Glue overlap at the point.

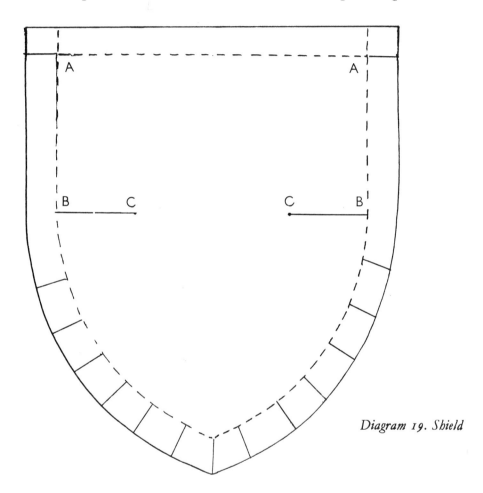

Diagram 19. Shield

To vary the size of the shield proceed as follows:

Draw a straight line A–A equal to the width of the shield required.

A–B = half A–A.   B–C = half A–B.

Draw lines A–B at right angles to A–A. Mark point C.

With the compass point at C describe the curves.

Cut a strip long enough to go round the sides, omitting the top, about $\frac{1}{4}"-\frac{1}{2}"$ wide. As this is a slow process it is advisable to glue only a small section of the folded edge at a time. Lay the shield face down and press the long strip to the glued edge keeping the edge of the strip and the scored edge of the border even. See diagram 20.

Chevron

In drawing the flat pattern the angle is wider than in the finished article as the scoring and folding make the angle more acute. Score the solid lines on the right side, the lower half of the vertical line—dotted in the pattern—must be scored on the reverse side. Glue small tabs behind the chevron marked X on the pattern. Very lightly mark a central line on the shield. Position the chevron on the shield so the centre point is on the line and the outer edges fit the curve on the outer edge of the shield. Glue, rub out the centre line. See diagram 21.

Cross

BEFORE CUTTING, score the horizontal and vertical lines, otherwise the point is difficult to fold. Score the dotted lines on the reverse side. Fold all lines carefully. Place the cross on the shield with a small dab of glue behind the centre.

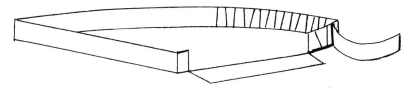

Diagram 20. Shield

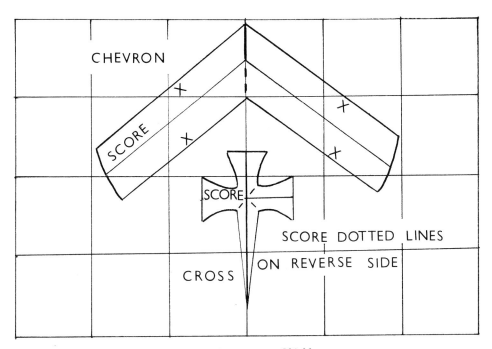

Diagram 21. Shield

HORSESHOE (Diagram 22)

Cut out the pattern and lightly mark the dotted lines. Score these on the right side. Cut the small lines round the edge to the scoring lines. Mark the nail holes on the wrong side, cutting the solid lines with a knife and scoring the dotted lines. Turn to the right side and gently push the cut sections through to the back. This gives a less stark look to the finished article than removing the sections altogether.

Fold all the cut edges back at right angles. Cut two strips of paper ½" wide, long enough to go round the outer and the inner edges. With a ruler lightly bend the paper along its length. Starting at the top outer edge run a little glue along a section of the folds. Lay the horseshoe face down on clean paper and press the strip onto the glued edge. See diagram 20 for the shield on page 51. Check to see that the lines are level with the scored edge. Continue round the outside edge, scoring the strip when turning at the top. Stop at the inner edge. Repeat the process with the inner edge again scoring at the turn, then overlap the first strip ending at the outer edge.

Embellish with roses on page 40 and ribbon.

Ribbon

Cut two strips of paper wider at one end than the other, and bend alternately on either side of the strip to give a rippled effect, as in photograph 13.

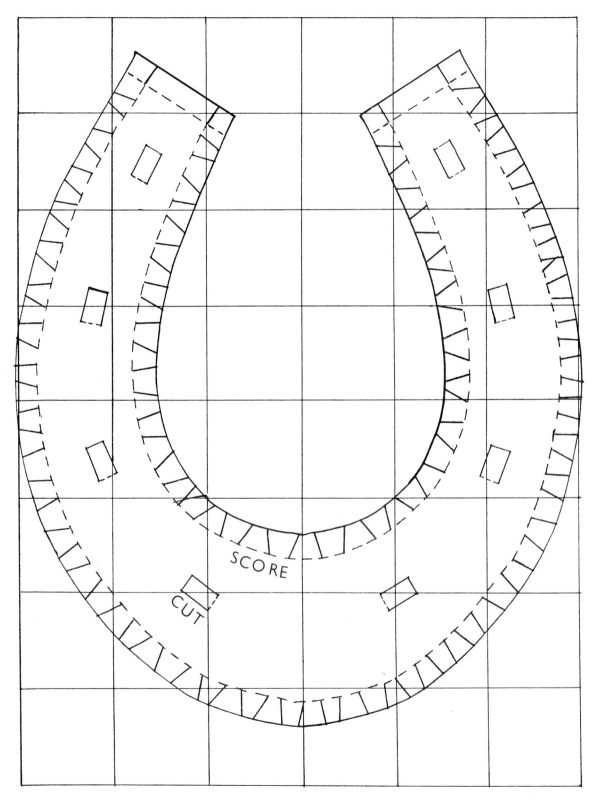

SCORE

CUT

Diagram 22. Horseshoe

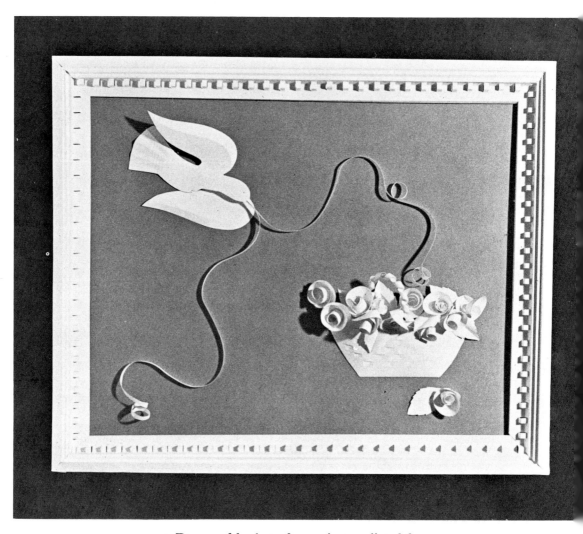

14. Dove and basket of roses in tessellated frame

DOVE & BASKET OF ROSES (Diagrams 23 and 24)

Dove

Cut out the pattern scoring as indicated. Fold the creases carefully especially the tail. Fold the lower wing pressing under the body at X (diagram 23). See the photograph on page 54.

Glue into position onto the background.

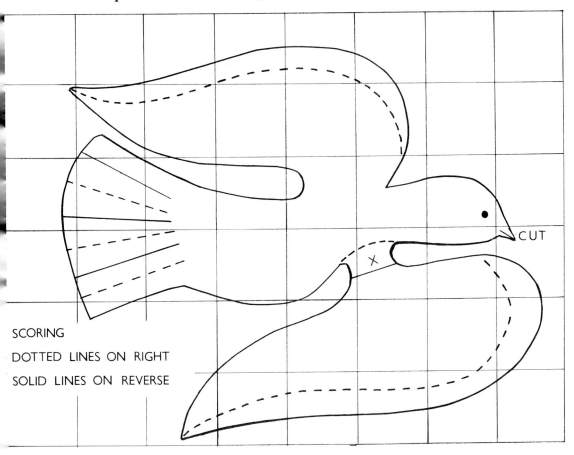

SCORING

DOTTED LINES ON RIGHT

SOLID LINES ON REVERSE

Diagram 23. Dove and Basket

Ribbon

Cut two long strips $\frac{1}{4}''$ wide. Bend with a ruler curling one end. Join the uncurled ends and fix in the beak with a dab of glue. Position the ribbon on the background fixing with small dabs of glue.

Basket

(Diagram 24 must be redrawn on to 1″ squared paper to get the correct size.)

Cut out the card structure, which is smaller than the basket or it would be seen in the finished picture (diagram 24).

Cut the basket shape and trace the pattern given. Score the solid lines on the right side. Cut the small lines to the scoring lines as shown.

Cut all the small horizontal lines with a fine trimming knife. Score the small dotted lines on the right side and the broken lines on the reverse.

On this side slip a small knife between the cuts and gently bend the paper as required. Bend the side and base edges back and fix behind the card structure, starting at the base. This will give a bowed shape to the basket. The upper tabs will be free of the card.

Cut a strip of paper 14″ × ¼″. Curl with the scissors and wrap tightly round a smooth pencil. Slip off the pencil and pull out from the centre twisting gently. Glue one end to the basket on the outside. Loop the handle over, fixing the other end to the card structure. Glue the whole to the background.

Fill with roses and leaves as described on page 40.

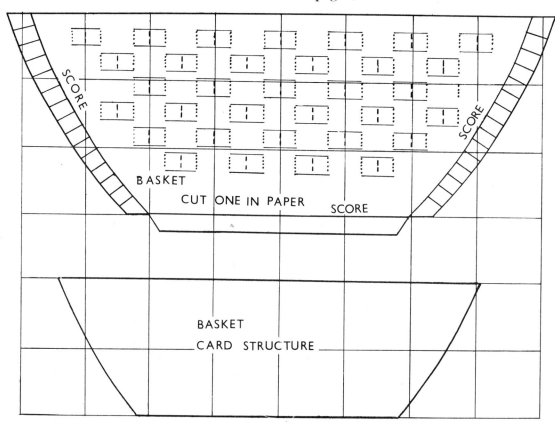

Diagram 24. Dove and Basket

15. Flying goose

FLYING GOOSE (Diagrams 25 to 31)

To enlarge this model redraw on $1\frac{1}{2}''$ or $2''$ squares. To make up either the given size or the larger, be sure that the card main structure, the body and bottom wing sections are each drawn in one piece putting the marks || ||| |||| together. Thus making three complete sections—diagrams 25 to 28.

Cut the main structure and wing structure in card. (The larger the size the stronger the card must be.) Glue the wing structure to the main structure as marked.

Cut the main body in paper and score all the dotted lines on the right side. Cut the eye very carefully and score the arch above the cut and across the base of the eye. See diagram 31 (1). Gently push through the cut section on the scored base line. Then carefully the arch. This will only give very little at the apex but the cuts at each end of the arch will give more easily. Practise on a rough piece two or three times as it is essential to keep this clean and smooth.

Now shape the beak and neck and head by folding along the dotted lines as shown on the pattern—diagram 27.

Cut small strips of paper and glue them to the back of the paper body at the places marked O. See diagram 31 (2). When dry and firm score the tabs on the right side close to the paper line in order to bend them to the back.

Try the paper shape over the card structure and trim the card if necessary.

Glue the neck tabs and fix behind on the card structure, being careful to retain the neck shaping. Repeat with the remaining tabs taking care not to pull them too tightly so causing the paper to bend.

Score across the line on the curved wing. Cut the feathers at the tip and fold back. Bend the wing with a ruler on the reverse side to give the curved flying effect. Glue and fix to the main body as shown—diagram 31 (3).

Cut, score and pleat the bottom wing section. Fix two tabs to the reverse side at the top. Lay over the card structure and fix tabs at the back. Repeat for the middle wing and fix at the top outer edge of the bottom wing as seen in the photograph on page 57.

Cut the top wing section, cutting the feathers with the trimming knife. Score. Again fix tabs to the back. Do not fix to the wing section yet.

Cut the top covering of the body. Score on the reverse side and bend the centre section on the reverse side with the ruler.

Cut the feathers with the trimming knife.

Place in position with the front point lying on the scored neck line—diagram 31 (4).

Top wing section slips into the cut in the body covering piece with the top end curve of the wing touching at the top—diagram 31 (4). This may need some manœuvring around to get the positions correct, as different scoring alters the shape. Glue where the wing goes into the cut and again at the neck.

Fix tabs on the wing to the back.

Score and pleat the tail. Fix tabs to the back—diagram 31 (5).

Glue each end of the tail—marked X on the pattern. Hold firmly in position until dry—diagram 31 (6).

Glue tabs to the card structure on the back—diagram 31 (7).

Score and shape the leg. Glue the leg and fix under the wing as shown in the photograph on page 57.

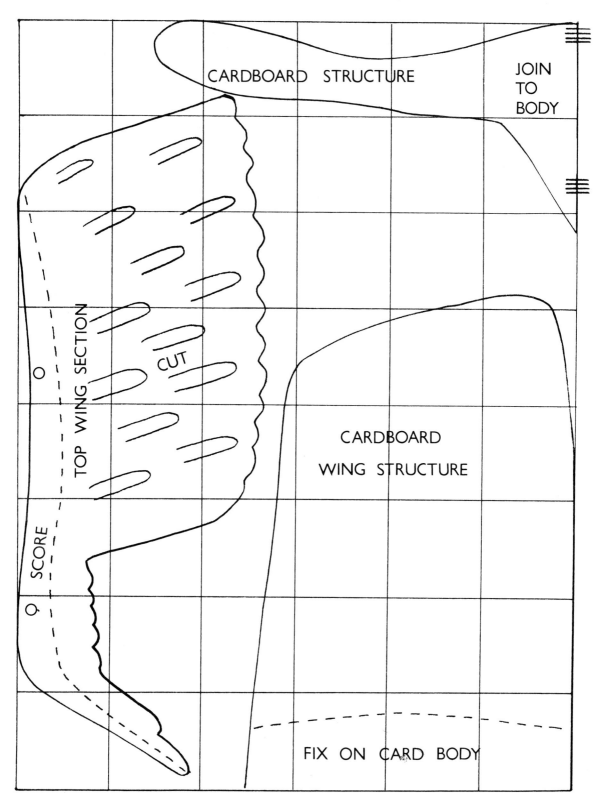

CARDBOARD STRUCTURE

JOIN
TO
BODY

TOP WING SECTION

CUT

SCORE

CARDBOARD

WING STRUCTURE

FIX ON CARD BODY

Diagram 25. Flying Goose

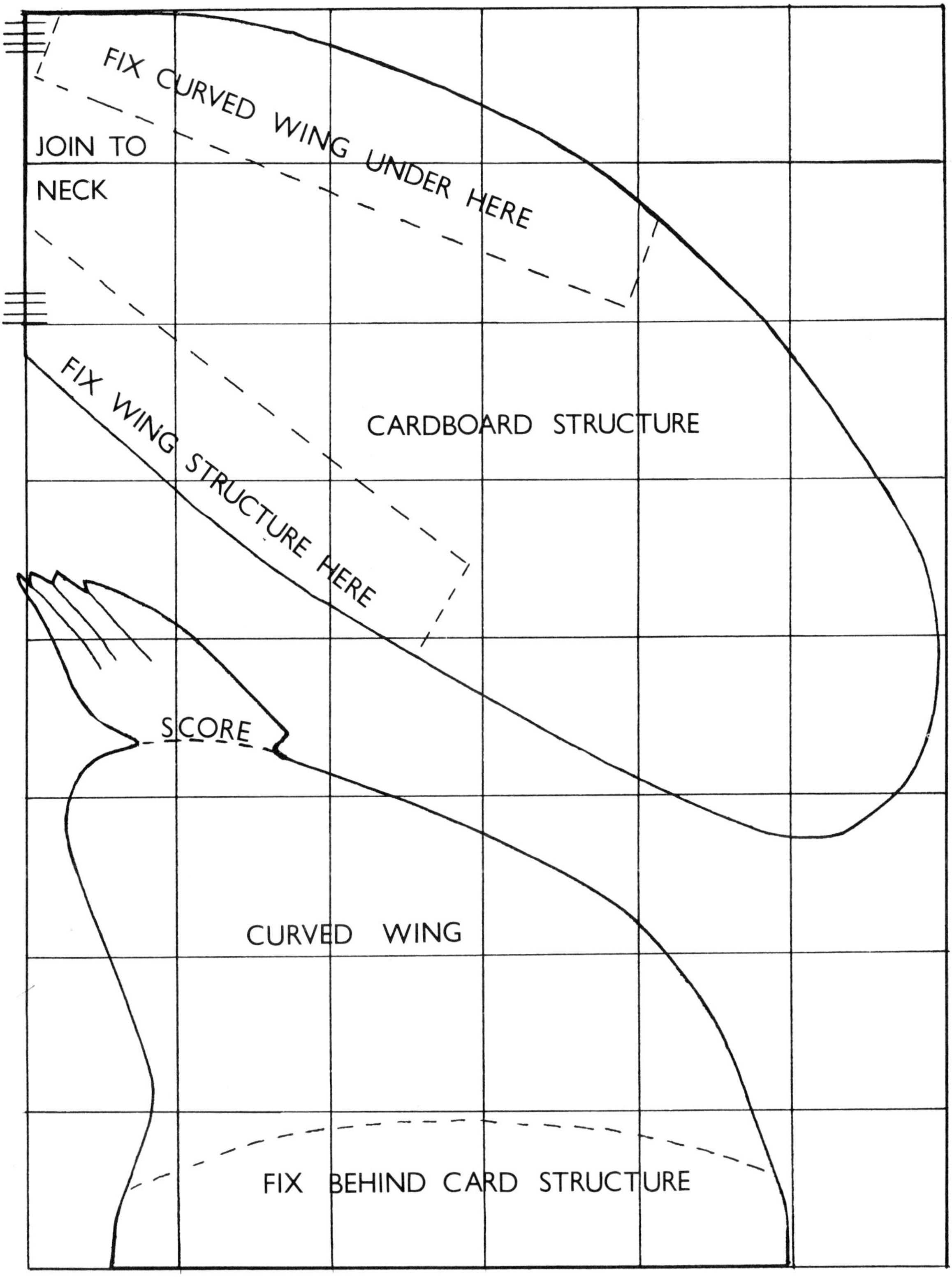

FIX CURVED WING UNDER HERE

JOIN TO

NECK

FIX WING STRUCTURE HERE

CARDBOARD STRUCTURE

SCORE

CURVED WING

FIX BEHIND CARD STRUCTURE

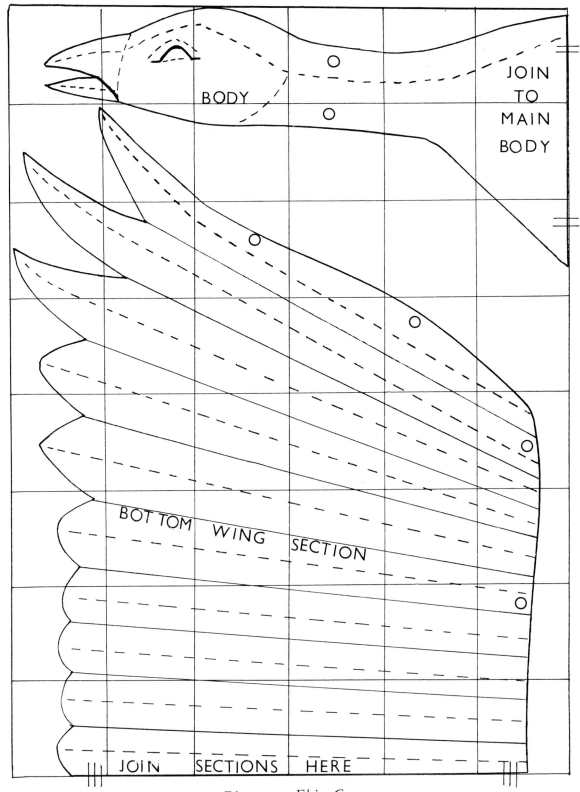

BODY

JOIN
TO
MAIN
BODY

BOTTOM WING SECTION

JOIN SECTIONS HERE

Diagram 27. Flying Goose

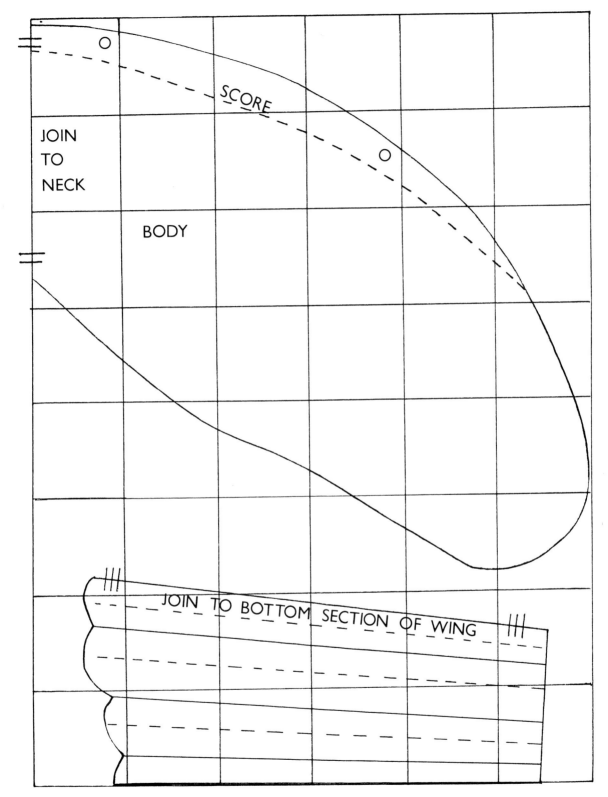

JOIN
TO
NECK

BODY

SCORE

JOIN TO BOTTOM SECTION OF WING

Diagram 28. Flying Goose

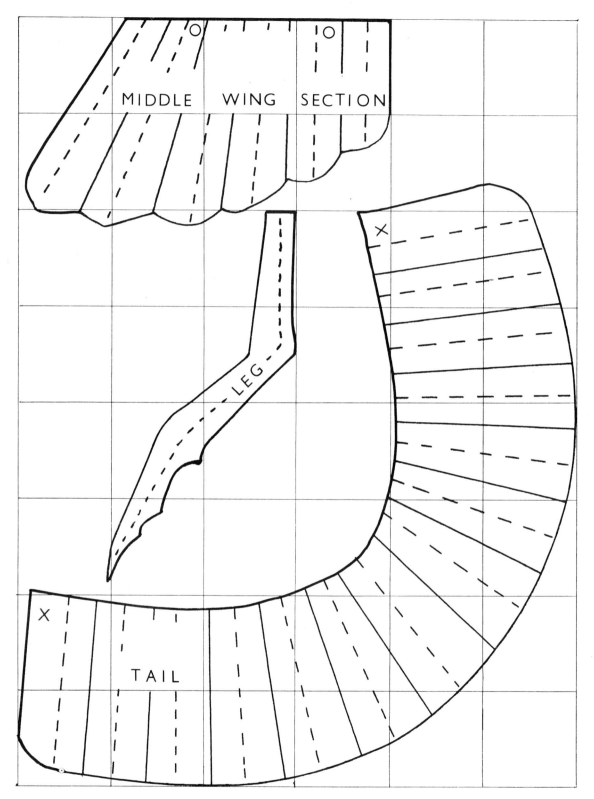

Diagram 29. Flying Goose

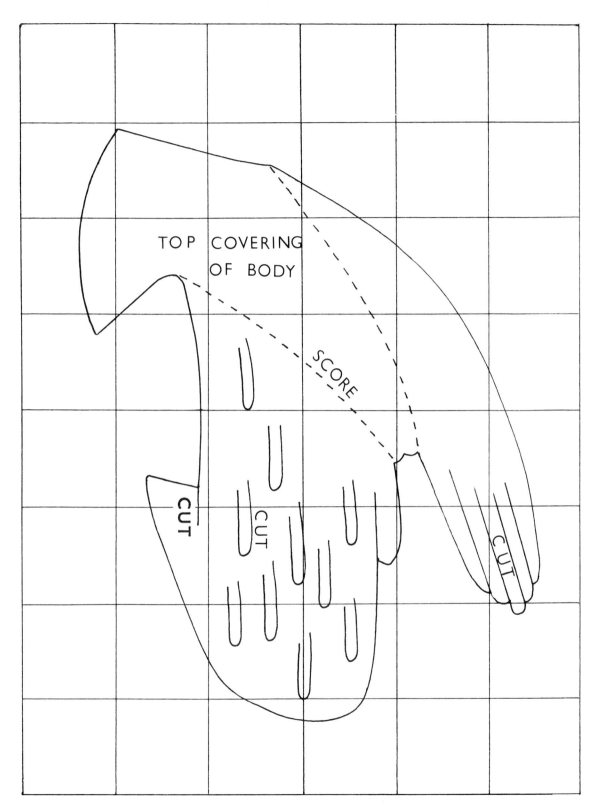

TOP COVERING
OF BODY

SCORE

CUT

CUT

CUT

Diagram 30. Flying Goose

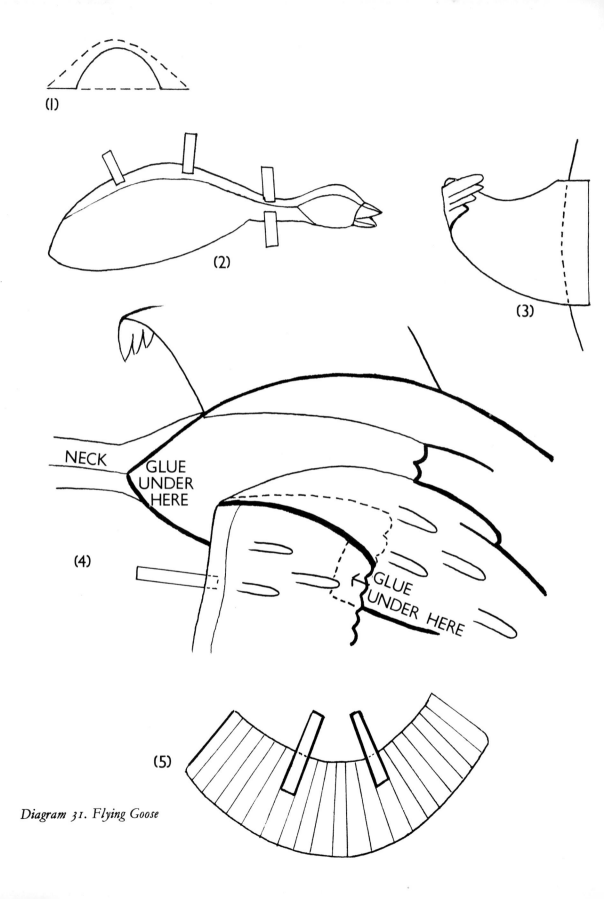

(1)

(2)

(3)

NECK

GLUE
UNDER
HERE

(4)

GLUE
UNDER HERE

(5)

Diagram 31. Flying Goose

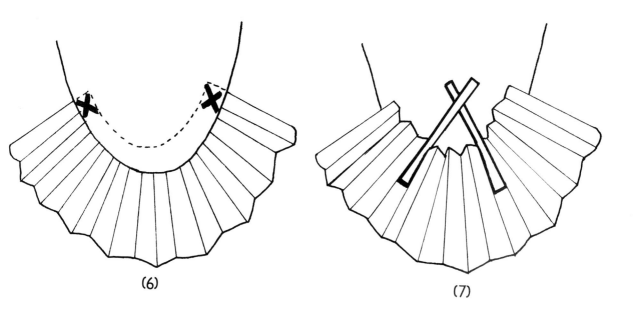

(6)   (7)

Diagram 31. Flying Goose

16. Heraldic lion in plain frame

HERALDIC LION (Diagrams 32 and 33)

This is made in a very simplified form but can become more elaborate with separate limbs and greater detail to the fur, etc.

RE-DRAW ALL THE PATTERN PIECES ON 2″ SQUARED PAPER. Cut out the structure in one piece in cardboard JOINING THE LEG TO THE BODY AT |||. Cut out the main body in one piece in paper, JOINING THE NECK TO THE BODY AT ||.

Score all the dotted lines on the right side and the solid ones on the reverse. Fix tabs behind all the places marked X. Score across these tabs on the right side along the paper line.

Position the foreleg A over the structure A covering all the cardboard, bend the tabs and fix behind the structure. Repeat the process with the hind leg B.

On the main body piece shape the outline of the shoulder and hip along the score lines indicated. On the reverse side slightly curve across the paper between these lines with a ruler. Position over the structure and fix as previously.

With the head cut away the eye section—marked in black in the pattern—with a sharp knife. Place in position fixing the tabs behind the structure.

Cut a long strip for the tail as seen in the photograph, spiralling—see page 12—a section to make the loop. Cut and score a shape for the tassel.

Glue the structure and fix to a background mounting card. Fix one end of the tail behind the lion and the rest to the background with a dab of glue here and there.

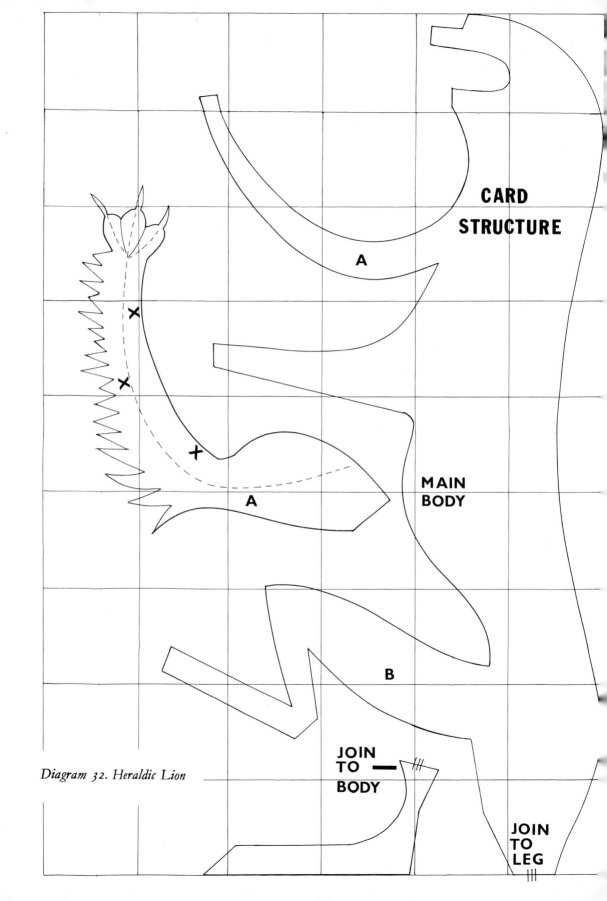

CARD
STRUCTURE

A

MAIN
BODY

A

B

JOIN
TO
BODY

JOIN
TO
LEG

Diagram 32. Heraldic Lion

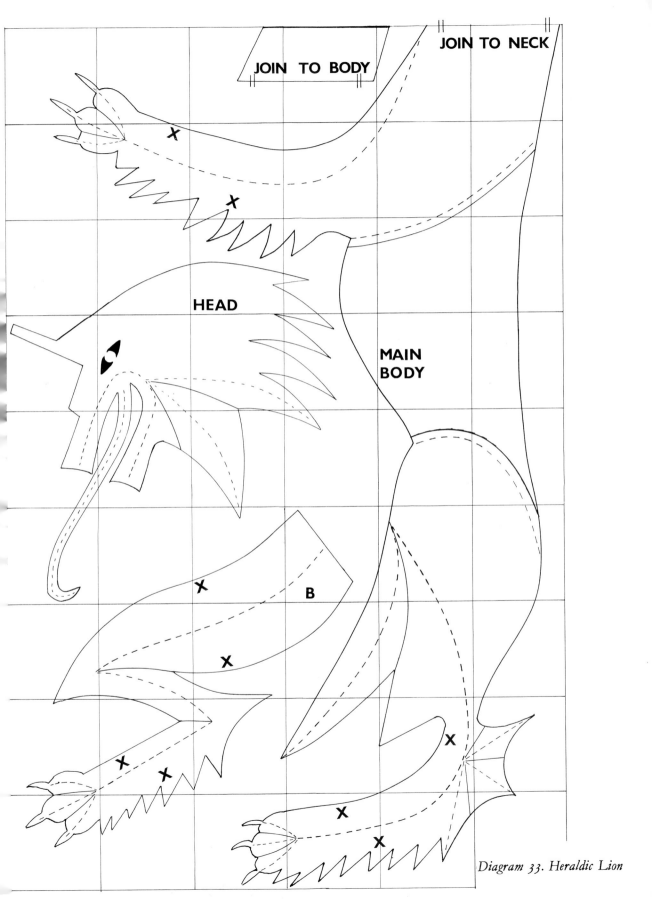

JOIN TO BODY

JOIN TO NECK

HEAD

MAIN BODY

X

X

X

X

B

X

X

X

X

X

X

X

Diagram 33. Heraldic Lion

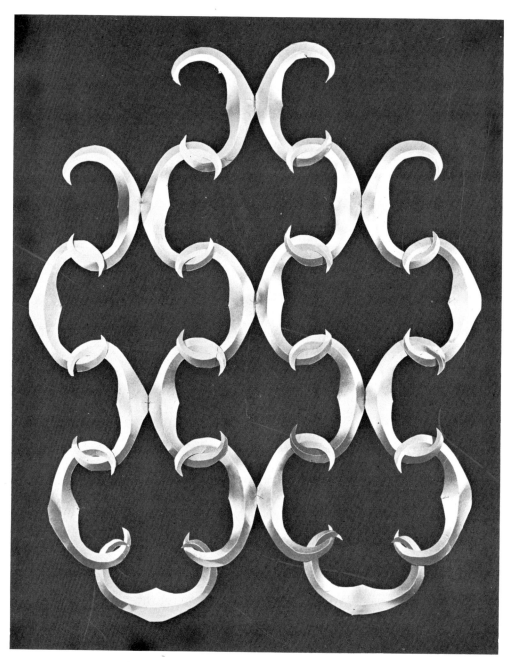

17. Gilded screen

GILDED SCREEN (Diagrams 34 and 35)

As scoring spoils the surface of foil-covered or painted cardboard, it is best to make up the pieces in a light cardboard, then spray paint them afterwards. Make a template from the pattern in diagram 34, then trace and cut out as many single sections as required.

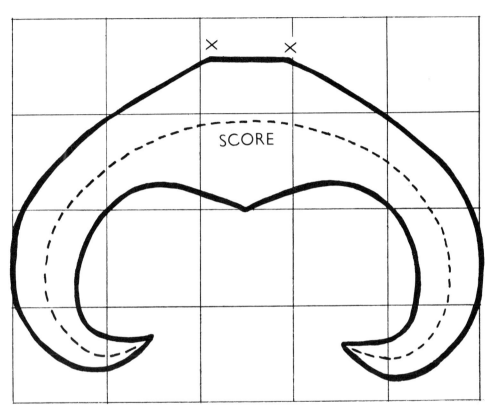

Diagram 34. Screen

Score on the line indicated on the right side. To keep the curve in shape, cut a small strip of cardboard the required length, adding $\frac{1}{2}''$ at each end. Score, and bend these extra pieces back and glue them to the back of the main section. See diagram 35.

Double Sections

Place two single sections 'back to back' with the curves facing opposite

74

directions. Place a strip of cardboard across the retaining strips and fix with a hand stapler or glue.

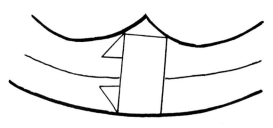

Diagram 35. Screen

4: Advanced Patterns

SHAKESPEARE (Diagrams 36 to 39)

This is a little more advanced, but having made several of the other items on the previous pages you should not find this too difficult.

Redraw the patterns on 2-inch squared paper to get the same size as the original—diagrams 36 to 38.

The neck measures $10'' \times 8\frac{1}{2}''$. With your ruler bend the paper across the 10″ length. Glue down one side and overlap $\frac{1}{2}''$. The neck will now stand 10″ high. Cut out the head section. Cut along the solid lines at the top removing the small triangles. With your trimming knife cut the curved lines for the cheeks. On the wrong side with your ruler bend the paper across the face. On the right side bend the cheeks to the front of the face.

Roll the face and glue the side seams to the back of the head making a 1-inch seam. See diagram 39 (1). Making sure the head is half an inch higher. Slip the head over the neck column and glue the back of the head to the back of the column. The face will now stand clear of the neck in the front.

Cut out the forehead as indicated in the pattern and score either side of the nose on the right side. On the wrong side with your ruler bend the paper across the forehead. Cut the solid lines at the top and above the eyelids to join the scoring at the top of the nose. Then gently bend the eyelids on the wrong side. Fold the score lines on the nose.

Glue the straight outer edges of the forehead and place on the assembled head. See dotted lines on the head pattern. Take care not to lose the shaping of the nose. Fix the nose in place by putting a little glue on a small strip of paper then carefully slip the glued end under the nostrils. Remove the slip and gently press the nose in place. Hold in position until dry. Take great care not to let any glue show.

Cut the eye sections from the pattern.

Then cut 2 strips $\frac{1}{8}'' \times 1\frac{1}{2}''$. Curl with your scissors and join into small circles. With a very small touch of glue place on the eye sections as indicated in the pattern. Fix in place under the eyelids so that half the eye is covered by the lid.

Cut out the eyebrows and cut the curved lines. Curl gently on the wrong side and place over the curled lids, so that the edge of the brow joins the scoring line on the nose. The outer edge of the brow covers the cut edge of the forehead.

18. Shakespeare

Hair

Cut the left hair piece A and REMEMBER TO REVERSE the pattern for the right piece. Cut all the solid lines and curl the hair on the wrong side at the base with your scissors. Hold the strips carefully so as not to tear them off. Cut and glue the lines at the top as shown. Gently bend the two end strips of the forehead towards the centre and place the hair piece approximately 2″ above the base of the second strip. See diagram 39 (2). Repeat with the right piece. Cut a small strip three to four inches long and glue one end to the bent back forehead section, fixing the other to the back of the head. See diagram 39 (3).

Cut the main back hair piece cutting all the solid lines as shown in the pattern. Overlap and glue the top lines to the dotted lines as indicated. Curl the ends of the hair as before. Fix this piece over the retaining strip and enclose the two side pieces. Hold until the glue is dry. Cut out the extra side pieces B and curl the ends, also curl the top to bend over the head.

Bend over the next forehead strip and glue the extra side piece in place over this strip covering overlap of back and side hair pieces. Repeat on the other side. You may find that one side is a little more difficult than the other as it is not easy to get two sides exactly the same.

Cut the final piece No. 2 and treat as before. Gently bend the last forehead strips back towards the centre, leaving the centre strip free and taking care to keep the dome shape glue the strips in place as they overlap. Bend back the central strip and glue in place over the top of the last hair section.

You may find you need small extra strips of hair pieces to cover any gaps, as no two models turn out the same. But by now you will be able to alter this and adapt for yourself.

Cut the moustache and beard, individually tapering each strand to a point. Place in position as shown in the photograph on page 76.

Cut out the collar and cut up the solid line as shown. Also cut away the centre circle. Score the outer circle, then cut and bend the tabs down. With a ruler lightly curl the collar points on the wrong side. Fit onto the neck column and overlap the back seam about $\frac{1}{2}$″ at the outer edge. Pull the collar up as you do so to keep the shape. Position the collar approximately 2″ up the neck at the back and $1\frac{3}{4}$″ in the front. Mark the place lightly with a pencil, and push the collar up a little higher. Then put a little glue round the neck on the pencil line, drop the collar into place and hold it until dry.

Although it is not shown in the photograph, make a box lid to give the model stability. This measures 10″ × 10″ × 3″. Cut a hole in the centre as for the collar, glue the tabs and put the neck in making sure the points of the collar are standing free from the box.

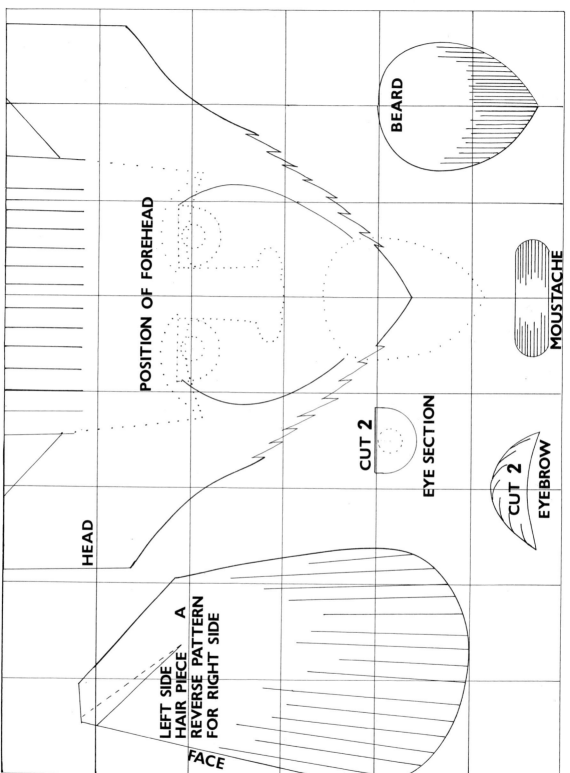

POSITION OF FOREHEAD

HEAD

BEARD

MOUSTACHE

CUT 2
EYE SECTION

CUT 2
EYEBROW

LEFT SIDE
A
HAIR PIECE
REVERSE PATTERN
FOR RIGHT SIDE

FACE

Diagram 26, Shakespeare

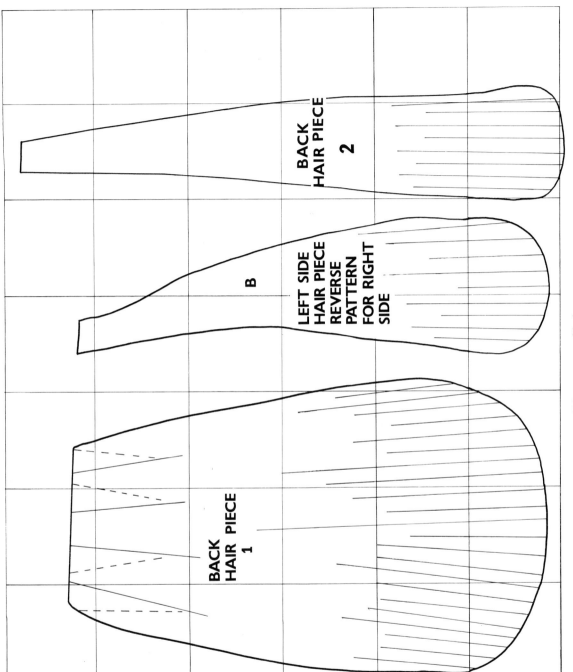

BACK
HAIR PIECE
2

B

LEFT SIDE
HAIR PIECE
REVERSE
PATTERN
FOR RIGHT
SIDE

BACK
HAIR PIECE
1

Diagram 37. Shakespeare

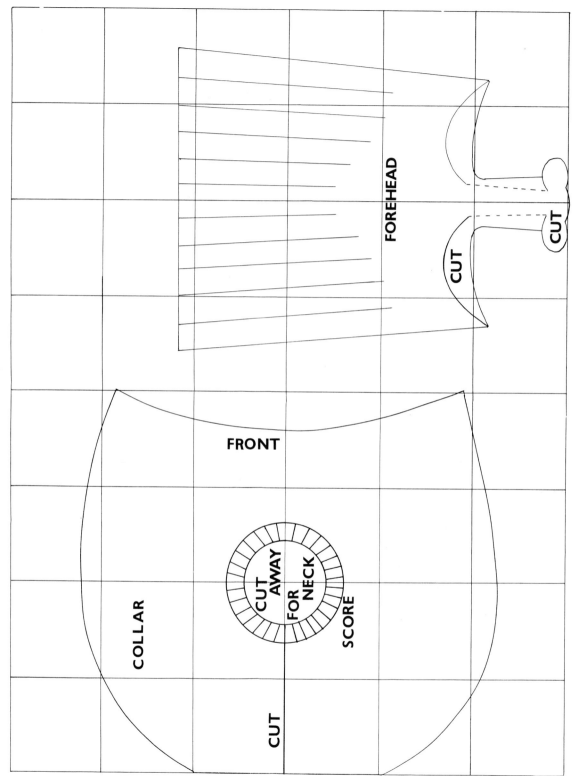

FOREHEAD

CUT

CUT

FRONT

COLLAR

CUT AWAY FOR NECK

SCORE

CUT

Diagram 38. Shakespeare

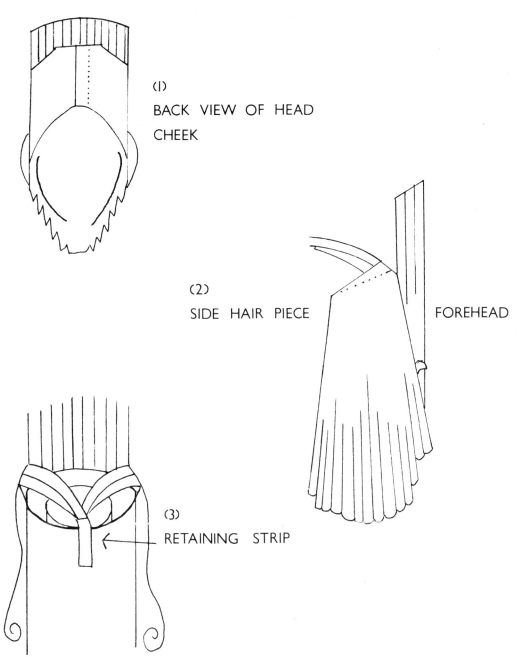

(I)

BACK VIEW OF HEAD

CHEEK

(2)

SIDE HAIR PIECE

FOREHEAD

(3)

RETAINING STRIP

Diagram 39. Shakespeare

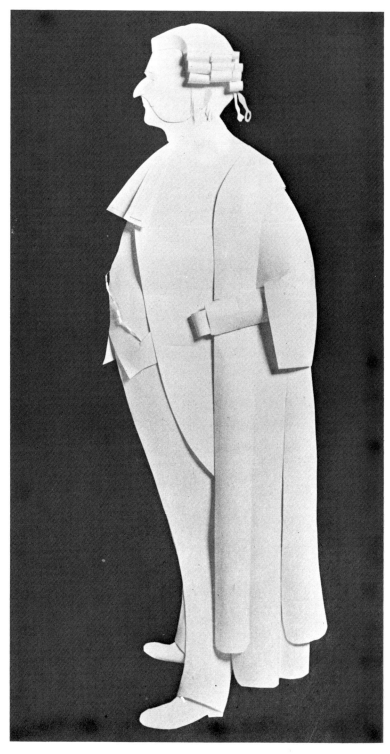

19. Barrister

BARRISTER (Diagrams 40 to 43)

Do study the pattern very carefully before you begin, as the pieces shown in diagrams 40 and 41 have to be redrawn onto 2″ squares to get the right size. Some pattern pieces have been drawn over others, but they have all been labelled.

Main Structure

Join the pieces A to B and cut them out in firm cardboard as one piece.

Right Shoe

Curl it across the length on the wrong side and add a tab above and below the shoe at X. When dry score all tabs across the paper line. Glue the tabs and bend behind the structure.

Right Trouser

Curl the length on the wrong side and score across the tab on the right side. Position by placing the end over the shoe on dots shown on shoe pattern. Glue and fix the tab behind the structure. Glue the top of the trouser to the structure.

Left Shoe

Score on the wrong side and gently crease. Curl across the length, then add tabs as for the other shoe. Glue the back of the heel to the structure and the tabs at the back.

Left Trouser

Add tabs at the places marked X. Score all the tabs and bend back. Curl across the lower end of the trouser on the wrong side. Position so the lower edge of the trouser is a fraction above the heel. Glue the lower tabs behind the structure, then the top tab and finally the others. Glue the top inner corner onto the structure and behind the calf, keeping the fullness in the leg.

Waistcoat

Cut along the solid line and overlap as shown on the pattern. Add two tabs at X. Position so Z is placed just below the trouser waist. Fix the tabs behind the structure and glue the inside straight edge to the structure keeping a slight fullness.

Head

Cut out the complete head shape and stick carefully over the cardboard structure. Over a pad of paper score the mouth with a blunt knife.

Face Relief

Score all lines shown on the pattern on the right side. Gently shape. Cut from the eye to the scoring line as shown. Bend the tab A–B and fix behind the structure. Leave until the nose is in place.

Nose

Cut the curved solid line at the end of the nose. Position so the squared end slips under the face relief, then keeping the cut piece free glue into place. Now the point C on the face relief slips into this cut. Glue it in place. Glue the upper inner curved edge onto the head shape.

Collar

Cut this yourself from a slightly curved strip about $\frac{1}{4}''$ wide. Only a very small section is visible. When you have the size suitable bend the ends and glue behind the structure. It will slope from the hair line to the base of the throat.

Coat

Score on a pad of paper with a blunt knife the four horizontal lines shown on the right side. Also score the shoulder on the right side and cut the small solid lines. Position so the coat almost covers the collar and falls away over the waist-coat showing about $\frac{1}{2}''$ of the cut. This serves as a pocket for the watch chain. Fix the shoulder tabs behind the structure. Put a dab of glue $1''$ above the coat tail on the straight edge.

Hair

Cut this piece separately from the head shape. Cut out the ear and score on the reverse side. Bend the ear forward slightly. Slash the hair as indicated, individually pointing the strands. Position on the head so the back curved edge covers the cardboard. Glue the rounded edge leaving the hair free.

Gown Folds

Cut out section D scoring the dotted line on the reverse side and the solid line on the right. Curl across the length either side of the scoring to shape the folds. Fix a tab at X. Position so the section is about an inch above the trouser end. See the photograph on page 82. Glue the outer edge from about $2''$ up to the structure. Bend the tab back and glue to the trouser.

Cut out section E. Curl the length on the reverse side. Fix a tab at X. Position so the fold is about an inch above the first section. Slightly off set the outer edge so it is off the structure. Fold the tab and glue to the back. Glue the top to the structure.

Cut the edge of the gown F. Score the broken lines on the right side. Cut the small and long solid lines, overlapping the long one onto the small dots. Glue. Fix over the edge of the shoulder, see the photograph, about $1\frac{1}{2}''$ from the neck. The fold falls over the first section and the trouser. A tab at X may be necessary.

Sleeves: Gown

Cut into the elbow on the solid lines shown. Score the broken lines on the right side. Fix a tab at X. Curl across the upper sleeve on the wrong side and also curl down the lower sleeve. Bend the scoring by the elbow cuts and glue to the area marked by dots. Glue underneath the upper curved edge then slip this under the gown edging at the shoulder. Fix the tab behind the structure. Cut out the sleeve and cuff section and score the solid lines on the right side and the dotted ones on the reverse. Curl across the length then pleat the cuff edge and fold this back along the score lines.

Cut a strip $5''$ long by $\frac{3}{4}''$ wide. Curl $1\frac{1}{4}''$ on the wrong side for the hand. Bend the scored edges of the sleeve and cuff and glue behind the strip keeping the centre of the sleeve and cuff rounded, and the cuff wider than the wrist. When dry glue the back and place the whole section under the elbow cuts in the gown sleeve and over the gown folds. See the photograph on page 82.

It may be necessary to slip a little glue under the gown edging here to stop the arm from sticking out too far.

Wig

Cut out and score the dotted lines on the right side. Cut the solid lines as shown. Fix the tabs at X. On the right side with your scissors curl the ends of the strips and roll closely. Position so the structure is covered. Glue the tabs at the back of the structure. Cut three strips $2\frac{1}{2}''$ long and as wide as the rolled strips. On the right side curl each end of each strip and roll to the centre. Place these above the curls already on the wig. Glue. Cut out two pig-tail shapes as in the photograph and glue them under the back curls. Make a small fourth curl and fix this over the pig-tail.

Bands

Cut out the two neck bands and cut two narrower strips and stick these on top of the larger ones. Glue the point of one band to the front of the collar. Tuck the point of the other band inside the collar front bending the rest of the band down so that it covers the coat edge. Glue to the coat edge.

Watch Chain

This is made from a very fine strip of paper which is twisted and pinched between the finger nails regularly along the length to give the chain effect. One end is glued into the cut in the waistcoat and the other behind the structure as seen in the photograph on page 82.

The other point of the waistcoat—no pattern given—is shaped and fixed behind the structure to match the edge at Z on the waistcoat.

Mount the whole figure by gluing the back onto strong mounting board of the required colour.

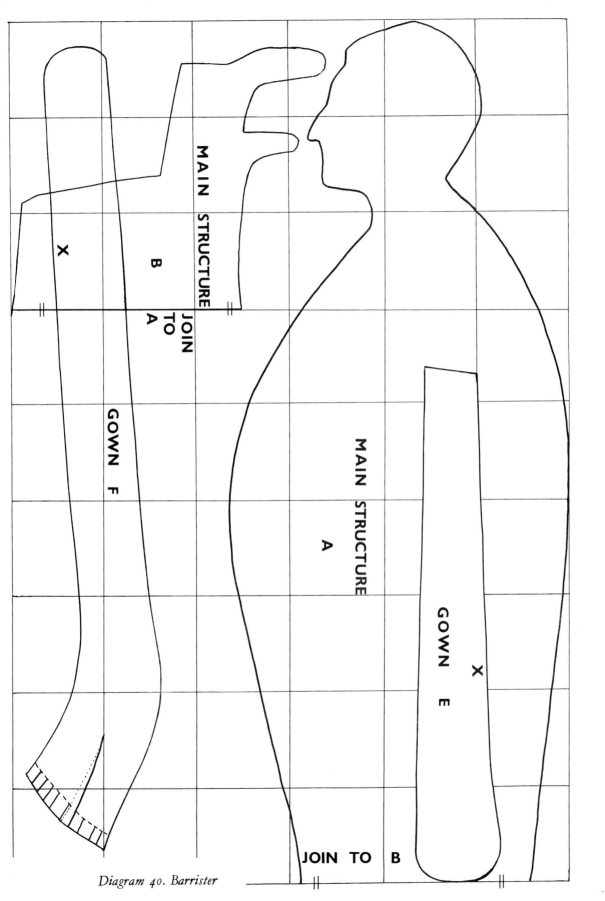

MAIN STRUCTURE
B
JOIN TO A

X

GOWN F

MAIN STRUCTURE
A

GOWN E
X

JOIN TO B

Diagram 40. Barrister

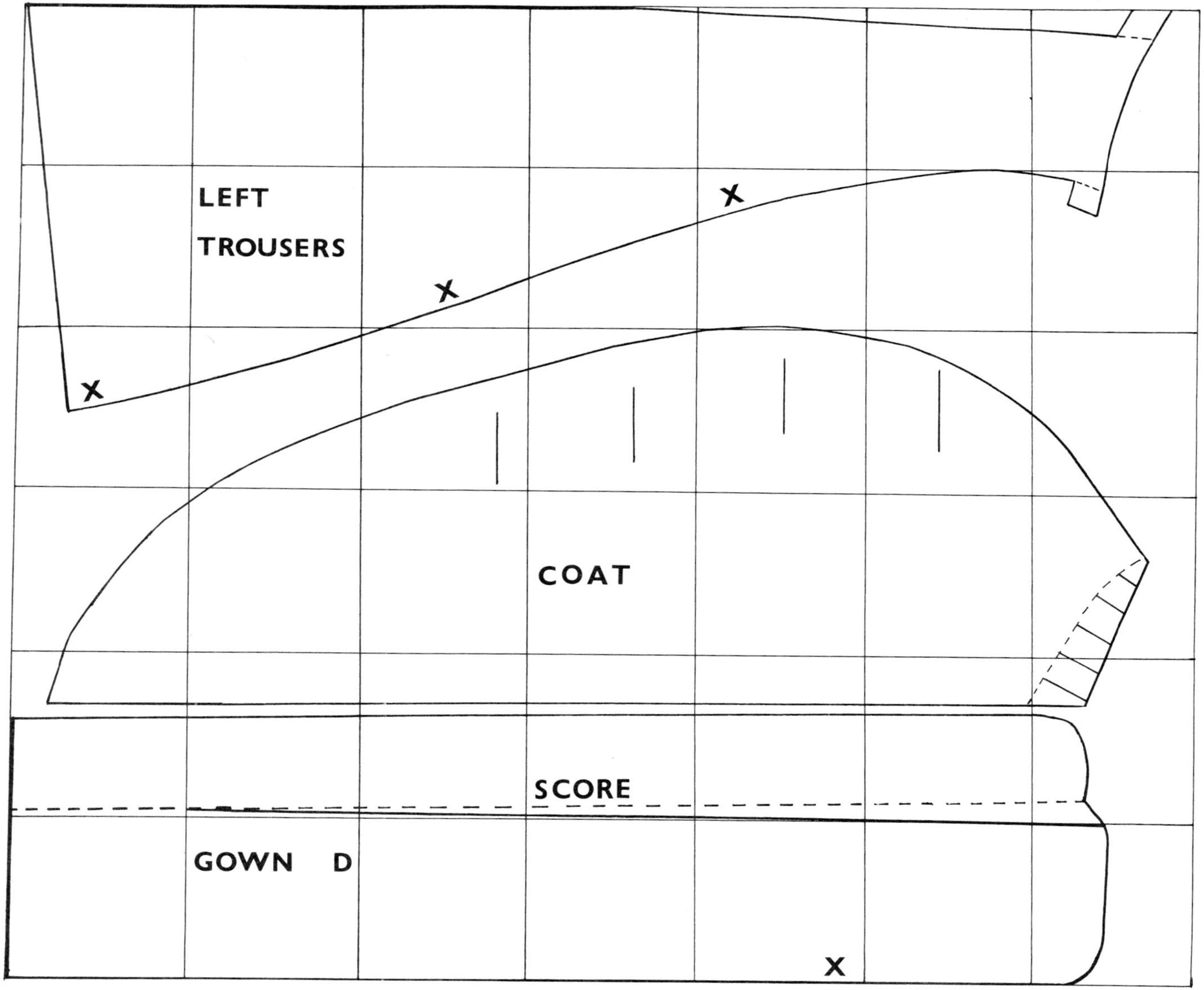

LEFT
TROUSERS

COAT

SCORE

GOWN D

Diagram 41. Barrister

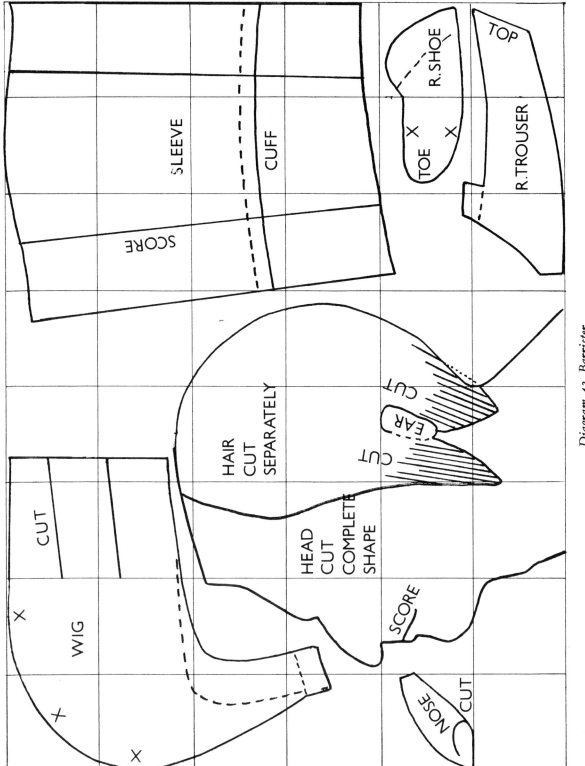

SLEEVE

CUFF

SCORE

R.SHOE

TOP

TOE

R.TROUSER

HAIR
CUT
SEPARATELY

EAR CUT

CUT

HEAD
CUT
COMPLETE
SHAPE

SCORE

CUT

WIG

X

X

X

X

NOSE CUT

Diagram 42. Barrister

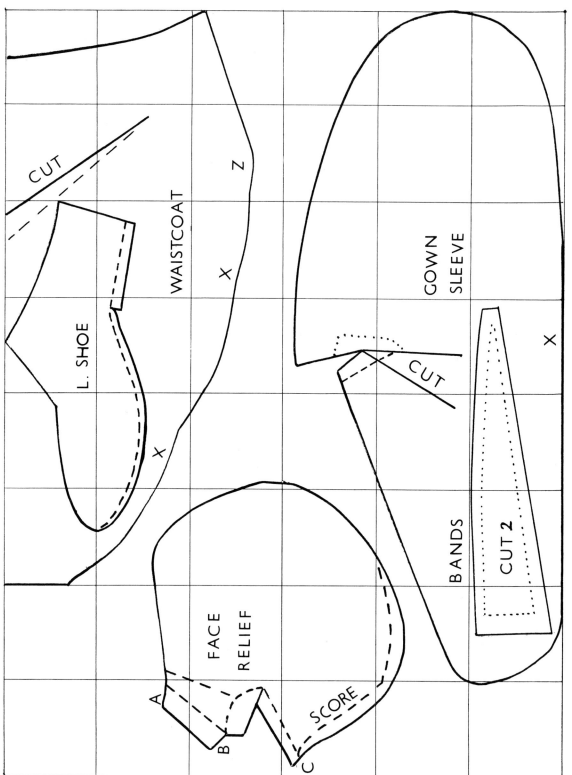

CUT

WAISTCOAT

Z

X

L. SHOE

X

GOWN
SLEEVE

CUT

X

FACE
RELIEF

SCORE

A

B

C

BANDS

CUT 2

Diagram 43. Barrister

PLAIN FRAME (Diagrams 44 and 45)

This is an easy and effective frame that can be used for photographs, notices, visual-aids, etc. It is mounted on strong cardboard and the photograph or coloured background paper must be fixed in place before making the frame. To hang a small picture it is possible to buy adhesive attachments, but for a large frame push a paper fastener through from the back and open the prongs on the other side, then cover with coloured paper, etc. Thread can then be tied here.

The difficulties of achieving an accurate method for a mitred corner are overcome by only shaping one end of each frame length, leaving the other straight.

Cut out the four frame sections to the required measurements, making sure the line C–D equals the dimensions of the cardboard. Score all the dotted lines on the right side and fold. See diagram 44. Work round the outside of the frame from right to left, keeping the shaped corner on the right.

Glue A–B–C–D on the underside and lay the cardboard on this, checking that the ends of the cardboard and frame meet exactly—diagram 45.

Fold under G–H–J–K and position along the area to be framed making sure C–D–F–E is in an upright position. Now turn the work so the next section on the left to be framed is in front. Repeat and glue A–B–C–D placing the cardboard

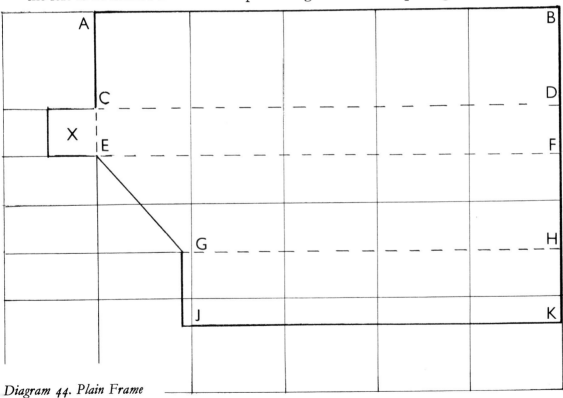

Diagram 44. Plain Frame

on top, keep the first section folded in position, fold the second section as before.

Make sure the mitre comes from the corner and goes over the straight end of the first section, then bend the tab X over the corner and glue to the first section. On a spare strip of paper put a dab of glue on one end and carefully slip this under the mitred section making sure no glue shows on the edge. Gently press to the first section.

Repeat this action all the way round. On a large frame the inside edge may lift slightly, if necessary slip a little glue under here and there as at the mitred corners.

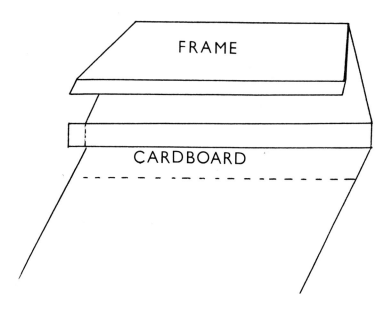

Diagram 45. Plain Frame

TESSELLATED FRAME (Diagrams 46 and 47)

This needs very careful measurement and scoring. Do not try to hurry. Cut all the lengths longer than needed. Make all pencil marks on the wrong side, a small pin prick can be made where necessary on the right side. See diagrams 46 and 47 and also the photograph on page 54.

Score the solid lines on the right side and the dotted ones on the reverse EXCEPT H AND J. These are measured along the length alternately in $\frac{1}{2}''$ and $\frac{1}{4}''$ spaces.

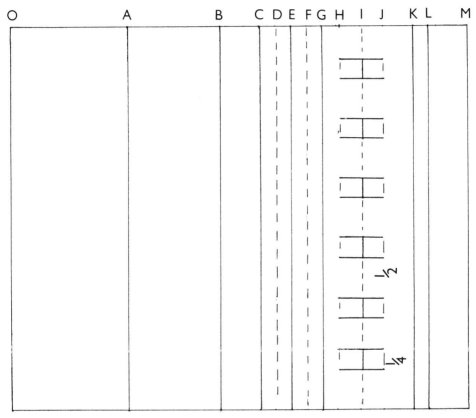

TENTHS OF AN INCH

$O-A = 1\frac{1}{2}$ $C-D = \frac{1}{5}$ $F-G = \frac{1}{5}$ $H-I = \frac{3}{10}$

$A-B = 1\frac{1}{5}$ $D-E = \frac{1}{5}$ $G-H = \frac{1}{5}$ $I-J = \frac{3}{10}$

$B-C = \frac{1}{2}$ $E-F = \frac{1}{5}$ $K-L = \frac{1}{5}$ $J-K = \frac{2}{5}$

$L-M = \frac{1}{2}$

Diagram 46. Tessellated Frame

Fold all the lines except H and J.

With a ruler and knife cut the horizontal lines indicated on the pattern. Score across each end of these cut strips on the wrong side, and across the centre of the strip on the right side. The rest of this line is scored on the wrong side.

Fold the lines G and K pulling them slightly towards each other, then push the small strips to the front and the pieces between to the back. This takes a while to manipulate and needs patience.

Mitre only one corner to make a close fit.

Position one length putting the section O–A behind the cardboard and repeat with another length making the corners even but leaving the other ends as they are. Cut the mitre carefully across on the horizontals and straight down the vertical sections. By not cutting the lengths to the correct measurements, if a mistake is made, there is enough length to try again.

Repeat the process at each corner.

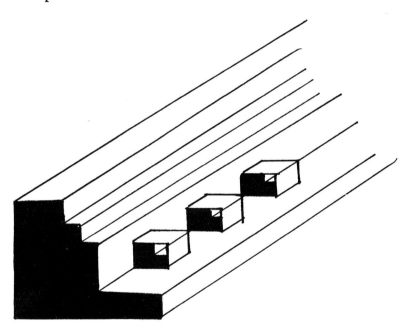

Diagram 47. Tessellated Frame

5: Christmas

CONE ANGEL (Diagrams 48 and 49)

Read the pattern carefully, DO NOT PLACE THE CENTRE LINE ON A FOLD, but trace round the pieces then carefully turn the pattern over keeping the centre in line—diagrams 48 and 49.

Make up the cone. See pages 22–23.

Cut out the sleeves, as in diagram 49, and gently bend with a ruler on the wrong side across the narrow centre with the short curved edge at the top, glue lower edge 2″ down from the neck of the cone on the seam line.

Cut out the wings and gently bend with the ruler across the centre on the wrong side. Slightly fold the wings back. Glue the centre over the sleeves and seam of the cone so the centre of the wings shows $\frac{1}{2}$″ above the neck of the cone.

Cut out the head. Lightly pencil the mouth and eyes on the wrong side, also on this side cut these with a knife very carefully to keep a clean line. Score across the top of the eyes still on the wrong side, then push the eyes to the front. Cut the top line, overlap and glue as shown. Glue the front of the neck tab and insert into the cone pressing against the front of the cone.

The angel can be made in white paper or coloured foil card for the cone, and gold or silver for the wings with the head in white. A small rectangle of folded paper to look like a carol sheet can be glued to the sleeves with tabs.

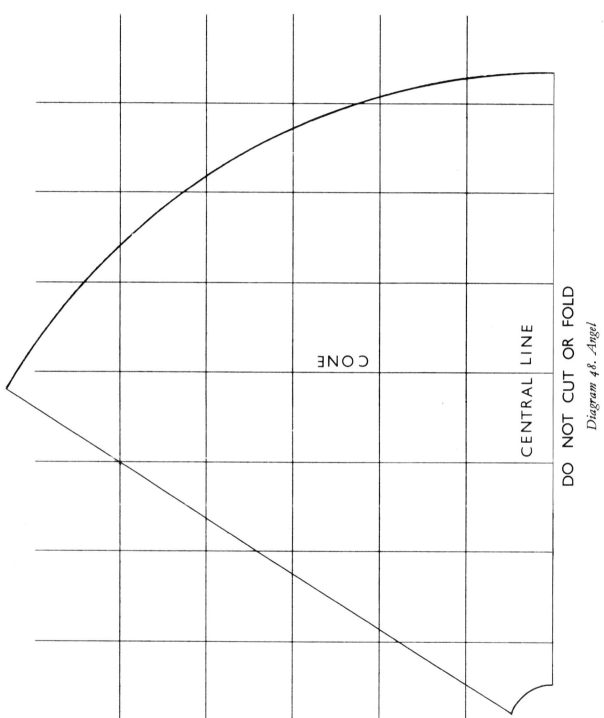

CONE

CENTRAL LINE

DO NOT CUT OR FOLD

Diagram 48. Angel

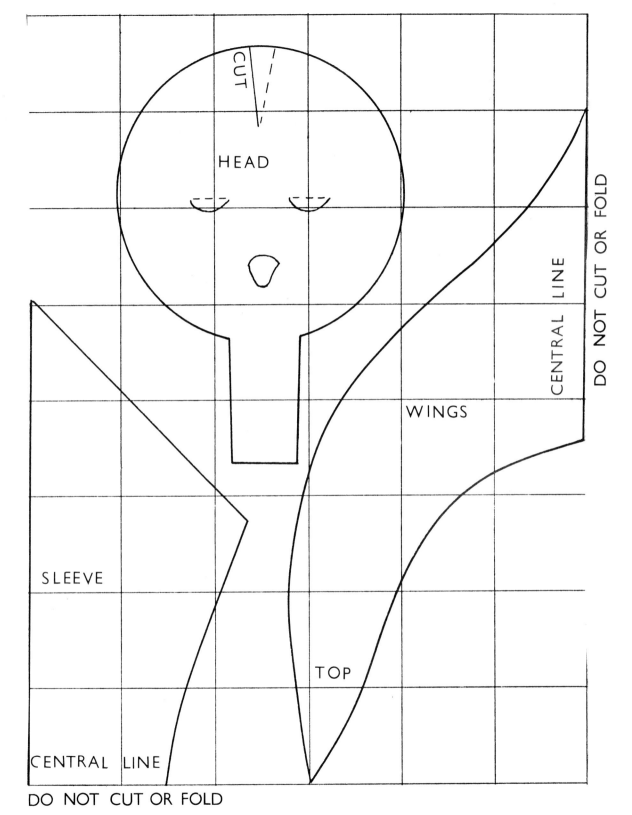

CUT

HEAD

WINGS

CENTRAL LINE

DO NOT CUT OR FOLD

SLEEVE

TOP

CENTRAL LINE

DO NOT CUT OR FOLD

Diagram 49. Angel

20. Christmas group 1—angel, reindeer and sleigh

REINDEER & SLEIGH (Diagrams 50 and 51)

Reindeer (Diagram 50)

Use cartridge paper for the given size and light cardboard for any larger size.

Cut the two pattern pieces taking care to place the neck and back edges on a fold.

Score the legs along the lines indicated on the right side. Gently fold.

Cut the fold line on the body from the neck end to X as shown on the pattern. Glue the neck between the body pieces on the lines indicated, slipping the folded neck edge into the cut along the folded body section.

Fold the head and glue the nose section together.

When dry open the body slightly to balance the reindeer on the legs. Open out the antlers. The body can be decorated with small spots from a gold doily. Another spot can be glued to hold narrow ribbon at the mouth for reins.

Sleigh (Diagram 51)

To make the sleigh the appropriate size for the reindeer, redraw the pattern onto 2" squared paper. Cut it out and trace round it onto a light cardboard. Keeping the central line X——X in position carefully turn over the pattern and trace the other half.

Score the lines A–B, C–D and E–F on the right side on the dotted lines only. The dotted lines G–H are scored on the reverse side. Fold all the lines separately. Fold the line A–B and trim the runners together with scissors.

Glue between the lines A–B and G–H on the wrong side. Fold the pieces together and hold until it is dry. Repeat with the other runner.

Fold the tabs 1. across the front of the sleigh. Bend up the tab 2. and glue to the tabs 1.

Fold the tab 3. across the back of the sleigh.

Bend up the tab 4. and glue to the tabs 3.

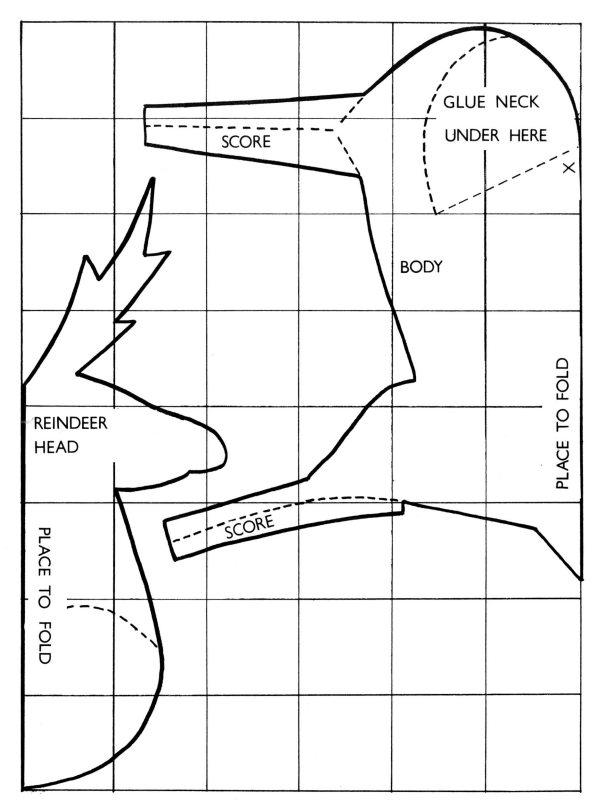

GLUE NECK
UNDER HERE

X

SCORE

BODY

PLACE TO FOLD

REINDEER
HEAD

SCORE

PLACE TO FOLD

PLACE TO FOLD

Diagram 50. Reindeer

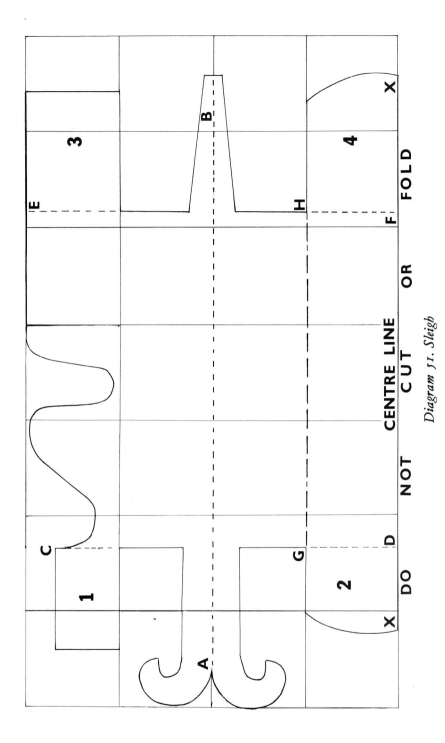

CENTRE LINE

DO NOT CUT OR FOLD

Diagram 51. Sleigh

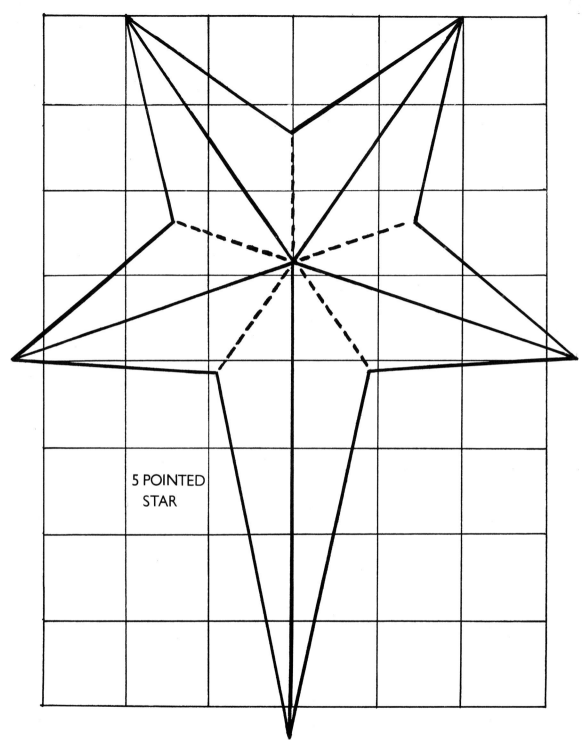

5 POINTED
STAR

Diagram 52. Five-Pointed Star

FIVE-POINTED STAR (Diagram 52)

This can be made to any size required in cartridge paper either white or coloured, gift wrapping foil, and light cardboard. Gold or silver spray paint can also be effectively used, either covering the star completely or just spraying the tips of the star. Further embellishments can be added by way of sequins, beads, pieces of gold or silver doilies, braids, glitter powders, etc.

To give an all-round effect, two stars can be placed back to back and glued at the points. A small hole pierced at the end of the scored line between the two top points and threaded with fine nylon thread will make the star hang with the long point downwards as in the pattern. It can also be hung from the long point. See diagram 52.

To Make:

Score the solid lines on the right side, and the dotted lines on the reverse. Crease all the folds carefully to the centre on the side they have been scored.

21. Christmas group 2—star and free-standing Father Christmas

FREE-STANDING FATHER CHRISTMAS (Diagrams 53 to 55)

1 sheet each of red, white and black cartridge paper 22″ × 30″.

CUT IN RED.

1 large cone, 1 small cone, 2 sleeves, nose and mouth.

CUT IN WHITE.

Head, beard, buckle, moustache, 2 strips $1\frac{1}{2}$″ × 30″.

CUT IN BLACK.

Base 11″ × 30″. From this cut a $\frac{1}{2}$″ strip from the long edge for the belt. The eyes are cut from the waste from the belt.

Body

Make up the large cone as in the earlier exercise. See pages 22–23. Take the long white strips and slash along the lines indicated cutting three-quarters across. Curl carefully with a knife, then roll a few at a time round a small smooth pencil. Glue around the base of the large cone on the right side. Stand the cone on the board and wrap a white strip of curled 'fur'—straight edge uppermost—over the glued edge and overlap on the back seam. Cut off the surplus. This will not lie flat as the cone is curved and the strip straight.

Sleeves

Repeat these processes on the sleeves.

Gently squash the top inch of the sleeves for easier fixing.

Keeping the seam of the main cone to the back, glue the sleeves, one at a time, $1\frac{1}{2}$″ down from the 'neck' at the 'sides'. These can be fixed with paper fasteners, but push them through the sleeve first. Then make a hole in the main cone, push through and open the prongs inside. Add a little glue as well.

Head

Cut the head piece along the lines indicated for the neck and hair. Roll, overlap along the short edge and glue the uncut edges together. When dry gather the neck strips into the hand to make an egg-cup shape. See diagram 55 (1). Run a little glue $1\frac{1}{2}$″ down the neck from the upper cuts, all round, also inside the neck on the main cone.

Holding the hair with one hand and keeping the neck gathers together with the other, poise it over the neck of the cone keeping the seams to the back. Quickly drop the neck into the cone and push it down well. Put one hand inside the neck and press the strips against the cone. Hold until dry and firm.

Bend the hair a little towards the centre.

Hat

Join the small cone (diagram 53) with paper clips and try on the head for size. The hat must fit tightly and cover the hair cuts. Then glue and fix the remaining fur. Run glue round the inside edge of the hat and fix to the head.

Beard

Cut the beard and slash as indicated. Curl with a knife on the right side. Glue the back of the beard at the top and fit it to the face at the sides close up to the hat and the lower edge to the lower face edge. No gap to show here.

Features

The correct size is shown in diagram 54. Score on the right side of the moustache and shape. Glue the top front of the mouth to fit behind the moustache. Glue the back of the mouth, fix it on the face so that the moustache covers the join of the lower face and beard.

Cut the nose to the centre, overlap $\frac{1}{4}''$ and glue to make a small cone. Carefully glue the rim and fix it above the moustache keeping the join line down the centre. Do not let any glue show.

Fix the eyes as indicated.

Cut the small square for the buckle, slash on the lines shown and thread the belt through. Overlap at the back letting the belt droop in the front, fit and glue the ends together.

Base

Roll the base and fix with paper clips. Adjust so that the large cone fits over it easily. Glue the edges of the base. Cut four 1″ tabs, and bend outwards as indicated. Glue the tabs and fit the cone over the base. Set straight and press the tabs to the cone.

Glue the top edge of the hands to the upper sleeve edge.

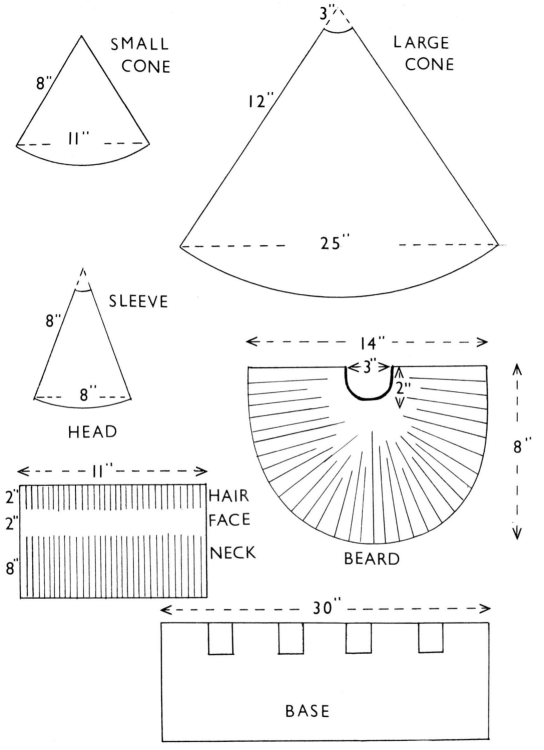

SMALL CONE

8"

11"

LARGE CONE

3"

12"

25"

SLEEVE

8"

8"

HEAD

11"

2" HAIR

2" FACE

8" NECK

14"

3"

2"

8"

BEARD

30"

BASE

Diagram 53. Free-Standing Father Christmas

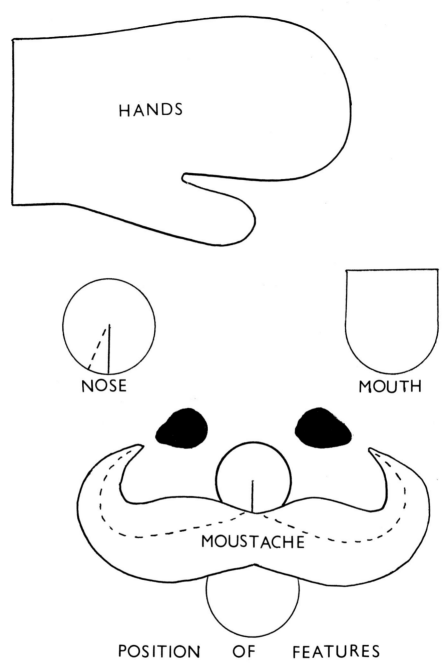

HANDS

NOSE

MOUTH

MOUSTACHE

POSITION OF FEATURES

Diagram 54. Free-Standing Father Christmas
and Waving Father Christmas
(the same features are used in both models)

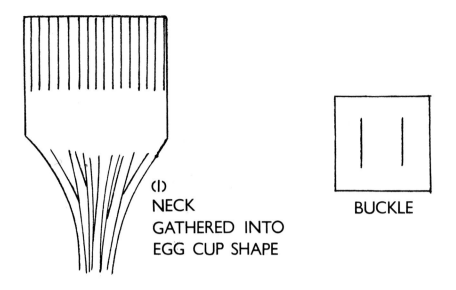

(I)
NECK
GATHERED INTO
EGG CUP SHAPE

BUCKLE

FUR

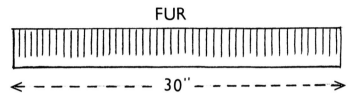

← - - - - - - - 30" - - - - - - - →

BASE ASSEMBLED

SHOWING TABS

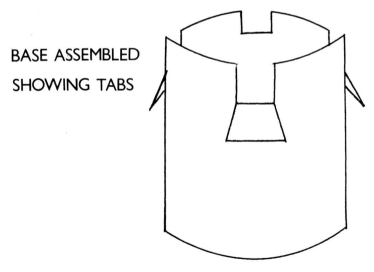

Diagram 55. Free-Standing Father Christmas

22. Waving Father Christmas

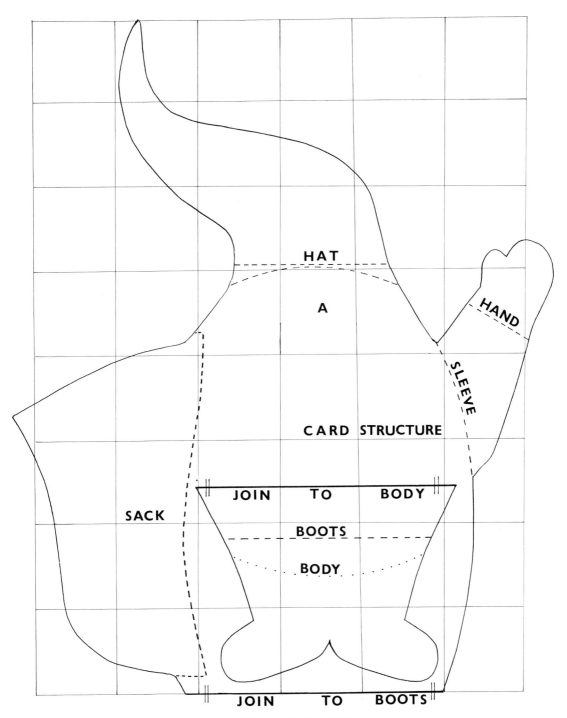

HAT

A

HAND

SLEEVE

CARD STRUCTURE

JOIN   TO   BODY

SACK

BOOTS

BODY

JOIN   TO   BOOTS

Diagram 56. Waving Father Christmas

WAVING FATHER CHRISTMAS (Diagrams 56 to 62)

Study the pattern carefully before cutting out the pieces. The diagrams MUST BE REDRAWN ON 2″ SQUARES TO GET THE CORRECT SIZE. The cardboard structure must be in one piece, so join the boots to the main section before cutting out. The sack and hatband are upside down in the pattern to fit into the pages.

Firm cardboard 22″ × 14″ for A.

Red cartridge paper for D.C2 E.G1. nose and mouth.

White cartridge paper for C1. C3. F1. F2. G2. G3. eyebrows, moustache, buckle and a strip 1″ × 11″ for the coat edging.

Black cartridge paper B.H.G4. eyes and a strip $\frac{1}{2}$″ × 11″ for the belt.

Cut out the cardboard structure.

Hand (Diagram 57)

Glue C1 to the hand on the structure to the line shown.

Left Arm

C2. Score across the tabs on the right side and fold them to the back. With the ruler curve across the width on the reverse side. Glue the long tab on the upper arm behind the structure. Then the others behind the lower arm, keeping the roundness of the sleeve.

Left Cuff

C3. Score the lines on the right side, fold to the back and curve on the reverse side as before. Place over the top of the sleeve and glue the tabs behind the structure.

Sack (Diagram 58)

B. Score the tabs on the right side and fold them to the back. On the reverse side curve from the centre to the tab edge along the length. With a trimming knife cut the solid line for the sack opening. Glue the tabs behind the structure, then glue the inner edge to the card structure. Hold until dry to keep the roundness.

Body

D. Score all the tabs on the right side. Score the vertical line at the base on the REVERSE side; still on this side curve along the length of the body and on each side of the vertical score line to shape the legs.

Cut the three solid lines then overlap and glue them to the dotted lines shown on the pattern. Glue the top tabs and fix them behind the structure at his shoulders, so the top curve lies approximately on the line shown on the structure. Check that the lower edge of the body comes to the dotted line at the base of the structure.

Glue the remaining unmarked tabs behind the structure taking care not to pull tightly, and that the score line for the legs goes inwards. Glue the tabs X, fold back and fix to the sack. To hold these down insert your ruler under the body and press the end onto the tabs.

Boots (Diagram 59)

H. Again score all tabs on the right side. Cut the solid lines on the feet. Score the centre line on the REVERSE side and fold. Curve on this side from the score line to the outer edges to shape the legs. Glue the heel tabs behind the structure making sure the top of the boots covers the edge of the body matching the centre score lines. Next fix the instep tabs, then the top ones and the next down. Add a small strip to the toe tabs and fix this to the back without pulling the toe which should stand clear.

Hat (Diagram 60)

E. Score the tabs on the right side. Curve across the width on the reverse side. Cut the solid line and glue to the dotted line shown. Hold the peak with a paper clip to the top of the card structure. Fix the tab at the end of the cut edge and glue behind the neck of the structure to line shown, then the opposite tab, keeping the roundness. Fix the outer tabs on the long curved edge watching all the time that the structure is covered. The inner tabs may need extra lengths added to prevent a strain.

Hat Band (Diagram 59)

F2. Score the dotted lines on the right side, curve on the reverse side. Check that the upward curve is uppermost, and fix over the end of the hat, keeping a high curve.

Beard (Diagram 61)

F1. Cut the curved and straight solid lines, gluing the latter to the dotted lines shown. Lifting the curved cuts, slip the top under the hat band. Glue the curves and press them onto the hat band. Score the moustache on the right side and shape. Use the pattern for the features on page 108 and place on the beard as shown by small dots on the pattern. The eyebrows come half on the face and half on the hat.

Coat Edging

Place the white strip over the cuts in the body, glue one end between the sack and the body and the other behind the structure on the other side.

Buckle and Belt

Cut a square $\frac{3}{4}''$ in white paper. Cut a $\frac{1}{2}''$ strip as on page 109. Thread the narrow black strip through the slits, slide the buckle to the middle, then fit the whole belt above the white coat edging in the same way.

Right Sleeve (Diagram 62)

G1. Score the dotted lines on the right side, and bend on the reverse. Fold the score lines and wrap the tab marked X right round the back and glue inside the sleeve at small dots marked in the pattern. This now makes a joined shaped circle.

Right Cuff

G.2. Score on the right side and bend on the reverse. Place over the cuff end of the right sleeve and glue the tabs behind Z.

Right Hand

G.3. Curve on the reverse side, glue in place with X to inside sleeve at tab X. Hand curls towards body. See photograph on page 110.

Sack Tie

G.4. Score the solid line on the right side and the dotted one on the reverse. Glue under the hand so that he holds it naturally.

Fixing Right Section to Body

Bend the remaining lower tab back, glue this and band Z placing the whole sleeve over the sack so the lower part of the sleeve is just above the level of the coat edging.

Make up small parcels in bright gay paper and tuck them into the sack opening.

Add a small circle of white paper for the pom-pom on the hat.

Made twice as big he makes a welcome to an entrance hall. The head and beard sections only, greatly enlarged, makes a cheerful motif for a Christmas fair or party. In this size the roundness is helped by gluing crumpled newspaper under the hat and upper beard.

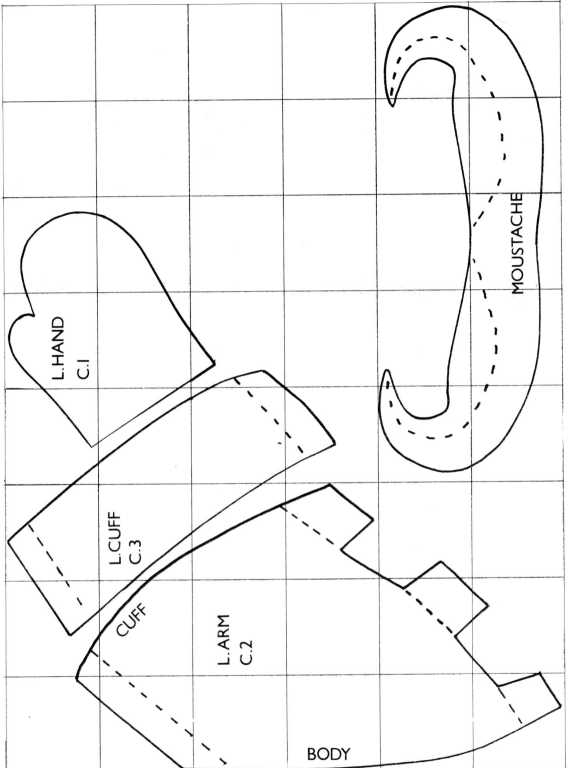

L.HAND
C.1

L.CUFF
C.3

CUFF

L.ARM
C.2

BODY

MOUSTACHE

Diagram 57. Waving Father Christmas

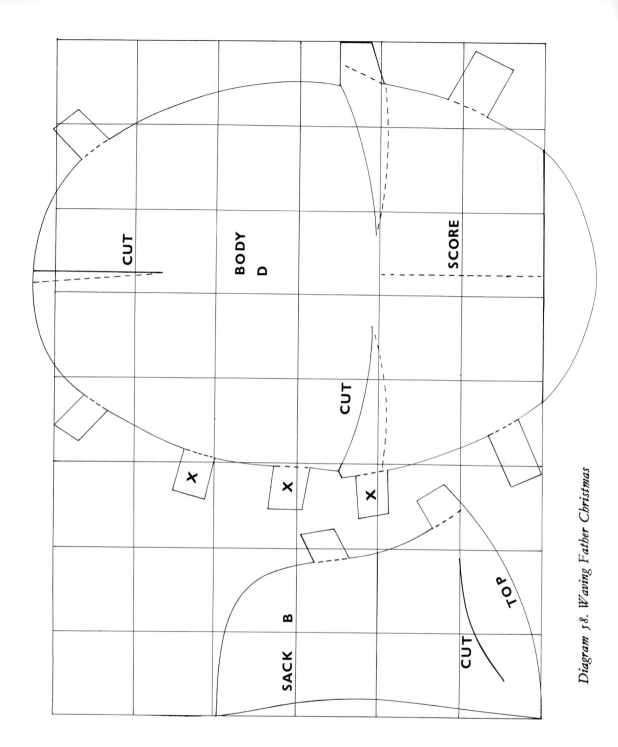

CUT

BODY
D

SCORE

CUT

X

X

X

SACK B

CUT

TOP

Diagram 58. Waving Father Christmas

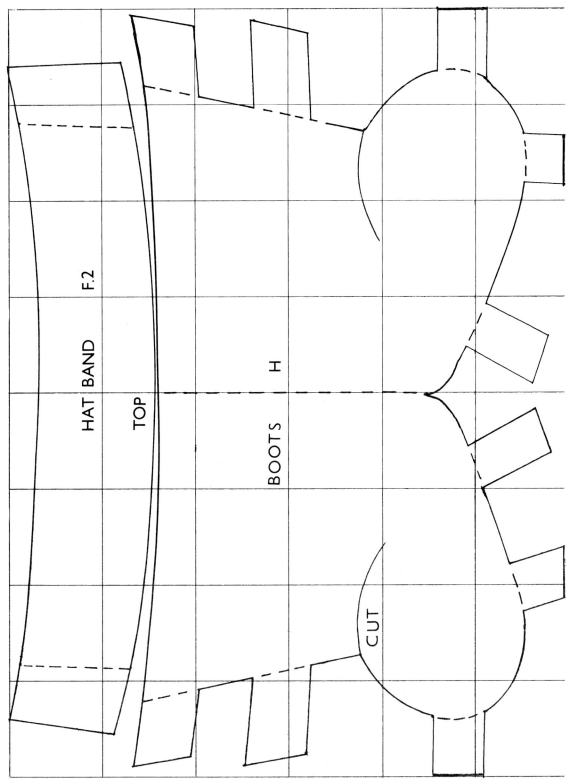

HAT BAND   F.2

TOP

BOOTS   H

CUT

Diagram 59. Waving Father Christmas

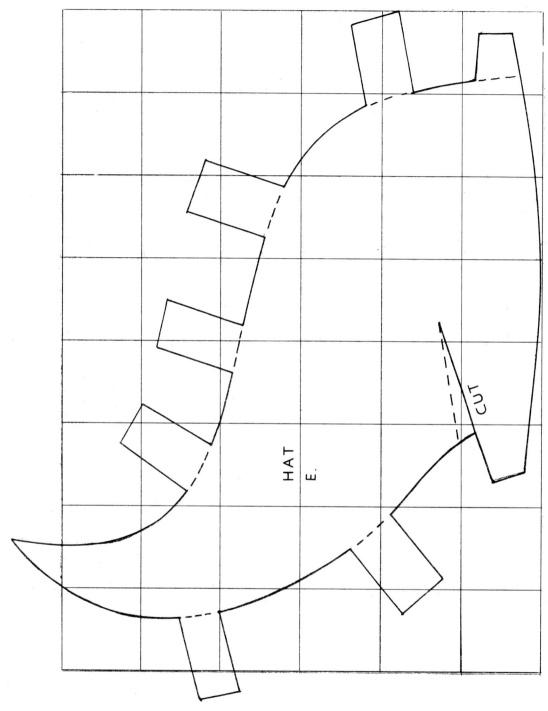

HAT
E.

CUT

Diagram 60

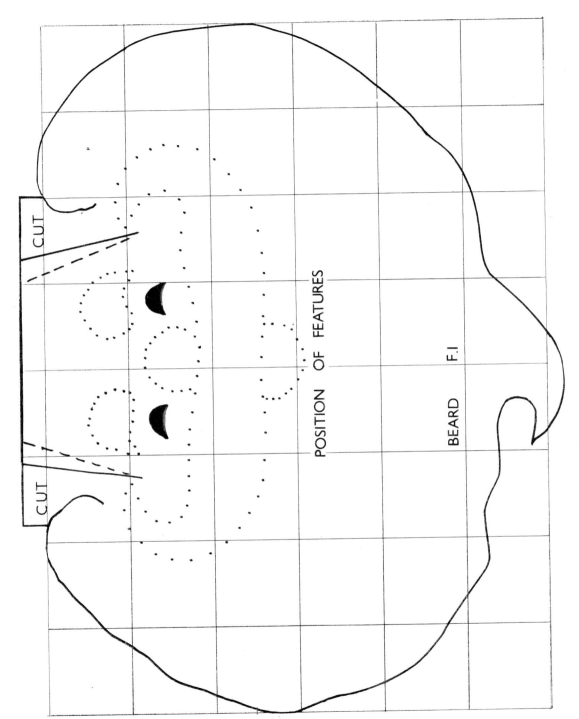

CUT

CUT

POSITION OF FEATURES

BEARD   F.1

Diagram 61. Waving Father Christmas

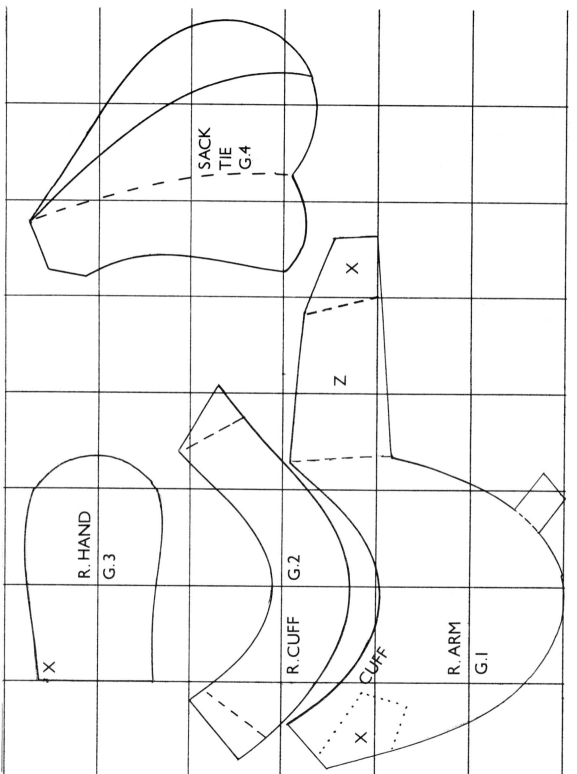

SACK
TIE
G.4

R. HAND
G.3

X

Z

X

R.CUFF
G.2

CUFF

X

R. ARM
G.I

Diagram 62. Waving Father Christmas

Paper Sculptue—Grand Opera

23. Madame Butterfly

Paper Sculpture—A Nursery Rhyme

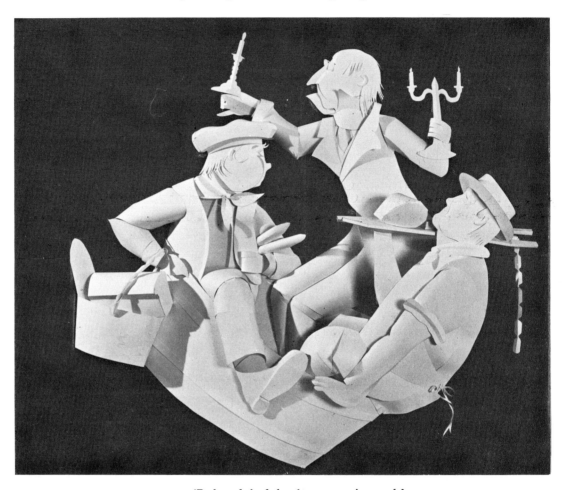

24. 'Rub-a-dub-dub, three men in a tub'